BIBLE TOP TENS

40 Fun and Intriguing Lists
to Inspire and Inform

BIBLE
Top Tens

40 Fun and Intriguing Lists to Inspire and Inform

Mary Elizabeth Sperry

Our Sunday Visitor Publishing Division
Our Sunday Visitor, Inc.
Huntington, IN 46750

ISBN: 978-1-61278-585-1 (Inventory No. T1281)
eISBN: 978-1-61278-211-9
LCCN: 2012932027

Interior design by M. Urgo
Cover design by Rebecca J. Heaston
Cover photo by Shutterstock

PRINTED IN THE UNITED STATES OF AMERICA

For my parents,
William and Katherine Sperry,
with my love
and undying gratitude.

CONTENTS

INTRODUCTION

I've always loved the Bible. It's one of the first books I can recall reading. (My parents had a wonderful picture Bible that was a particular favorite of mine.) The people, places, events, and language of the Bible have always drawn me. I was fortunate that my Catholic school education included an excellent foundation in Scripture, helping me to come to a fuller understanding of God's Word.

Understanding of and appreciation for the word of God is essential to a life of faith. We cannot grow in our love of our God if we do not know the story of God's love for us that is recounted in the Bible. In his Apostolic Exhortation *Verbum Domini*, Pope Benedict XVI teaches:

> A knowledge of biblical personages, events and well-known sayings should thus be encouraged; this can also be promoted by the judicious *memorization* of some passages which are particularly expressive of the Christian mysteries. Catechetical work always entails approaching Scripture in faith and in the Church's Tradition, so that its words can be perceived as living, just as Christ is alive today wherever two or three are gathered in his name (cf. *Mt* 18:20). Catechesis should communicate in a lively way the history of salvation and the content of the Church's faith, and so enable every member of the faithful to realize that this history is also a part of his or her own life. (#74)

This book is intended to help people build their knowledge of Scripture by organizing important people, places, and events into "countdown" lists. Lists can serve as a memory aid or provide ideas for further reading and study. Ideally, you will read this book with a Bible in hand, reading more about the stories that interest you most. To assist, I have provided Scripture citations where appropriate.

Keep in mind that the selection of these lists and their rankings are one person's opinion. If you disagree, write in your own selections and rankings. If you think I missed any important lists, tell me about them at bibletoptens@gmail.com.

This book can be used for personal reflection and study, as a way to direct your own Bible reading. Pick a list and read the stories that underlie the entries, praying about what these stories mean to you. There's no particular order in the listing, so you can feel free to skip around, following your interests. Teachers, catechists, and youth ministers might use these lists to help young people come to a fuller understanding of our faith history. And getting to know our ancestors in faith can serve as good examples or trenchant warnings! These stories are reminders that God's love is constant, even when we fall away.

My hope is that reading these lists will help people grow in their love of Scripture and draw them closer to the God who made us for love and union with him.

TIPS FOR THE FRUITFUL READING OF SCRIPTURE

The Bible is all around us. People hear Scripture readings in church. We meet the Good Samaritan (Luke 10), welcome home the Prodigal Son (Luke 15), and look for the Promised Land (Exodus 3, Hebrews 11). Some biblical passages have become popular maxims, such as "Do unto others as you would have them do unto you" (Matthew 7:12), "Thou shalt not steal" (Exodus 20:15), and "Love thy neighbor" (Matthew 22:39). But the Church also strongly encourages us to read Scripture at home. And today's Catholic is called to take an intelligent, spiritual approach to the Bible.

10. Bible reading is for Catholics. The Church encourages Catholics to make reading the Bible part of their daily prayer lives. By reading and reflecting on these inspired words, people grow deeper in their relationship with God and come to understand their place in the community to which God has called them in himself.

9. Prayer is the beginning and the end. Reading the Bible is not like reading a novel or a history book. It should begin with a prayer asking the Holy Spirit to open our hearts and minds to the Word of God. Scripture reading should end with a prayer that this Word will bear fruit in our lives, helping us to become holier and more faithful people. Pope Benedict XVI strongly promotes the ancient practice of *lectio divina* (divine reading). This practice combines the reading of Scripture with contemplation and prayer to strengthen Christian living.

8. Get the whole story! When selecting a Bible, look for a Catholic edition. A Catholic edition will include the Church's complete list of sacred books along with introductions and notes for understanding the text. (Protestant Bibles do not include seven books found in Catholic Bibles and two other books omit certain sections found in Catholic Bibles.)[1] A Catholic edition will have an *imprimatur* or canonical rescript on the back of the title page. An *imprimatur* or rescript indicates that the book is free of errors in Catholic doctrine.

7. The Bible isn't a book. It's a library. The Bible is a collection of 73 books written over the course of many centuries. The books include royal history, prophecy, poetry, challenging letters to struggling new faith communities, and believers' accounts of the preaching and passion of Jesus. Knowing the genre of the book you are reading will help you understand the literary tools the author is using and the meaning the author is trying to convey.

6. Know what the Bible is — and what it isn't. The Bible is the story of God's relationship with the people he has called to himself. It is not intended to be read as a history text, a science book, or a political manifesto (though the Bible does have much to teach us about history, the natural world, and relationships in the human community). In the

---

1. The books included in Catholic Bibles are Tobit, Judith, 1 and 2 Maccabees, Wisdom, Sirach, and Baruch. The Catholic editions of Esther and Daniel include sections omitted in Protestant Bibles.

Bible, God teaches us the truths that we need for the sake of our salvation.

5. The sum is greater than the parts. Read the Bible in context. What happens before and after — even in other books — helps us to understand the true meaning of the text. Taking a single line out of context may help to win an argument, but it won't necessarily help you understand God's message.

4. The Old relates to the New. The Old Testament and the New Testament shed light on each other. While we read the Old Testament in light of the death and resurrection of Jesus, it has its own value as well. Together, these testaments help us to understand God's plan for human beings.

3. You do not read alone. By reading and reflecting on Sacred Scripture, Catholics join centuries of faithful men and women who have taken God's Word to heart and put it into practice in their lives. We read the Bible within the tradition of the Church to benefit from the holiness and wisdom of all the faithful through the ages.

2. What is God saying to me? The Bible is not addressed only to long-dead people in a faraway land. It is addressed to each of us in our own unique situations. When we read, we first need to understand what the text says and how the faithful have understood its meaning in the past. In light of this understanding, we then ask: What is God saying to me?

1. Reading isn't enough. If Scripture remains just words on a page, our work is not done. We need to meditate on the message and put it into action in our lives. Scripture must inform *and* form us. Only then can the word be "living and effective" (Hebrews 4:12).

THINGS YOU SHOULD KNOW ABOUT THE BIBLE

Saint Jerome once said that "ignorance of the Scriptures is ignorance of Christ." Knowing both the contents and the context of the Bible are important to development in the life of faith.

10. The Bible is the most translated book in history. The Bible has been translated into almost every known language, and projects are underway to complete translations in the remaining languages. There are even groups who are translating the Bible into Klingon and Elvish — invented languages that no one speaks!

9. While the Bible was written down over the course of more than one thousand years, it covers a much longer period. While portions of the written text are much older, most of the Bible was actually compiled between the reign of King David in 1000 B.C. and the end of the first century after Christ's birth. It covers the period from prehistory through the patriarchs and Moses (about 1800 B.C.), through the rise and fall of Israel's monarchy, and through the deaths of the Apostles in the second half of the first century.

8. Many of the human authors of the biblical books are unknown. Many of the books bear the names of traditional authors (such as the Wisdom of Solomon), but in many cases, the exact identity of the human author is unknown. What we do know is that the human authors and editors did their work under the inspiration of the Holy

Spirit, consigning to writing everything that God wished to communicate.

7. The way the word "Lord" is printed in the Bible means something. In the Old Testament, the word "Lord" is often printed as "LORD." When that print style appears, it means that the original Hebrew text uses YHWH, the divine name, in that place (also called the tetragrammaton since it is transliterated with four letters). Judaism has a longstanding tradition of never speaking the divine name. In the past, it was spoken only by the high priest in the Holy of Holies on the Day of Atonement. Since the destruction of the Temple in A.D. 70, this rite has not been possible. While the divine name is not reproduced in most Bible translations, the print style will let you know when it is used.

6. No single copy of the original Bible exists. People often ask where they can find the original Bible. The short answer is that such a text does not exist. Over the centuries, individual books of the Bible were copied by scribes to be shared. For example, Paul's letters to various churches were copied many times and shared in other cities. When translators begin to work a new edition of the Bible, they must first consult the work of scholars and archaeologists to determine which manuscripts are closest to the original. As more archaeological finds are discovered, our knowledge of the Bible's origins increases.

5. The original books of the Bible are in many languages. While most of the Bible was written in Hebrew and Greek, other ancient languages are represented as well, including early forms of Syriac. For the most part, the New Testament was composed in Greek, the scholarly language in the Roman Empire. Most of the Old Testament was composed in

Hebrew, though some books are available to us today only in a Greek translation, called the Septuagint, that predates the birth of Christ.

4. The books of the Bible are not printed in chrono-logical order. In the canonical order of Catholic Bibles, the books are divided by genre, not organized chronologically. Some books of the Bible retell stories from other books. For example, Deuteronomy retells much of what happened in Exodus and Numbers, and the Books of Chronicles retell the history of the Israelite monarchy from David to the fall of Judah. In other cases, different books tell the same stories from different perspectives. The best examples are in the Gospels, though the prophetic books often recount events also told in the Books of Kings and Chronicles.

3. In the Bible, the same person or place is often called by different names. The Bible can be very confusing since the same person or place often goes by different names. For example, Mount Sinai and Mount Horeb are the same place. The Sea of Galilee and the Sea of Tiberias are the same body of water. Reuel and Jethro are the same person, as are Abed-nego and Azariah and Jedidiah and Solomon. In some cases, a person's name is changed for religious meaning or for po-litical reasons. In other cases, the various names are a lasting reminder that various cultures and armies controlled this land, each naming people and places as they wished.

2. Three stages can be identified in the formation of the Gospels. The Gospels are neither contemporaneous accounts of Jesus' life nor are they biographies as we under-stand them today. The Church has identified three stages in the formation of the Gospels. The first stage was the life and ministry of Jesus — the actual teaching, healing, living, and dying of Jesus. The second stage was the Apostles' preaching about what they saw Jesus say and do. The Apostles' preaching always took place in light of what they knew about Jesus' death and Resurrection. The third and final stage was the consignment of this preaching to the written form that comes down to us today.

1. The Bible is salvation history. While the Bible contains history, it does not claim to be an historical record of the ancient world. While the Bible teaches about the natural world, it is not a scientific treatise. The Bible is the story of our salvation by a God who created us for love and who, in turn, loved us so much that he sent his Son as one of us to save us from death and show us the way to everlasting life.

BIBLE MISUNDERSTANDINGS

It probably comes with being the most read book of all time, but the Bible seems to be the most misunderstood book of all time as well. Our impressions of the Bible are often informed by art or by popular wisdom in ways that are not supported by the text.

10. A surprising number of people will cite "God helps those who help themselves" as one of their favorite Bible verses. There's just one problem: That saying isn't in the Bible. In fact, the sentiment it expresses is quite different from what the Bible teaches. God's grace does not depend on our initiative and efforts. God loves us even in our sinfulness and shows special care for those who are weak and unable to help themselves.

9. Another frequent Bible misquote is that "money is the root of all evil." The actual quote, in 1 Timothy 6:9–10, makes it clear that the "*love*" of money is the real problem. Wealth and material goods are neither good nor bad in and of themselves. How we relate to the things of this world and the priority we give them are the source of the problem. When we value things over God and other people, evil can flourish.

8. A variety of conspiracy theories attempt — incorrectly — to explain the choice of books in the Bible.

The official list of books in the Bible (called the canon) developed over the course of centuries. The list of books we know today was fairly well-established by the fourth century. Despite many theories to the contrary, the choice of books was not determined by political considerations. The key factors in determining whether a book was accepted into the canon were its widespread use in the Church and its compatibility with the Tradition of the faith.

7. Unlike the First and Second Books of Samuel, Kings, and Chronicles, the First and Second Books of Maccabees do not follow each other historically. Rather than telling two sequential parts of a larger story, the First and Second Books of Maccabees tell the same story from two different perspectives.

6. The Stations of the Cross are not a Scriptural devotion. Several of the stations, including the meeting with Mary, the three falls, and the kindness of Veronica, are not recounted in the Gospels. The Stations of the Cross developed out of the practice of pious pilgrims walking in the footsteps of Jesus as he approached his death on Calvary. As they walked the Via Dolorosa (the Way of Sorrows), they stopped to reflect prayerfully on Jesus' passion and death. When they returned home, they took the devotion home with them to share with their communities.

5. The Book of Genesis never says that Adam and Eve eat an apple. The specific type of fruit shared by Adam and Eve in opposition to the command of God is not identified. The text refers simply to the fruit of the tree of knowledge of good and evil and says that it looked good to eat. The idea that the fruit was an apple developed much later and spread widely through the common artistic depictions of the original sin.

4. There's no horse in the scene of Paul's conversion in the Acts of the Apostles. Despite popular depictions of Paul being knocked from his horse when he hears the voice of Jesus, the Bible text never mentions a horse. It simply says that Paul is knocked to the ground. Though Paul is traveling to Damascus on a commission from the high priest, it is extremely unlikely that a tentmaker like Paul would have access to a horse.

3. The Bible doesn't say that three kings visited the baby Jesus. The second chapter of Matthew's Gospel recounts the visit of magi from the East. A *magus* (the singular of magi) is not a ruler but a learned sage. Often, magi were skilled in astrology, explaining why these magi were following a star. The number three comes from the three gifts offered: gold, frankincense, and myrrh. Of course, gifts to givers may not be a one-to-one correspondence. Finally, the text tells us that the magi set out when they saw the star announcing Jesus' birth. Based on Herod's murder of all boys less than two years of age, Jesus was probably a toddler before the magi arrived.

2. The Bible does not predict the end of the world or identify the Antichrist. Periodically people will announce the day that the world will end or identify an individual as the embodiment of the Antichrist. Of course, their pronouncements are always based on "clues" in the Bible. However, the Bible never gives a name to the Antichrist. And, regarding the day that the world ends, Jesus clearly states that not even he knows the day or the hour. Only the Father knows. If the Father did not tell the Son, doesn't it seem unlikely that he told anyone else? Generally, these predictions and identifications tell us far more about the one making the statements than about the Bible.

1. The God in the Old Testament and the New Testament are one and the same God. Periodically throughout history, the claim has arisen that the God depicted in the Old Testament is a different, typically lesser, God than the God revealed by Jesus. God in the Old Testament is seen as jealous, punitive, and cruel, as contrasted with the loving and caring God in the New Testament. The Church has fought this view, always proclaiming that Scripture, Old Testament and New, reveals one true God in three persons: Father, Son, and Holy Spirit.

ONE

PEOPLE

"M" IS FOR THE MILLION WAYS ...

Okay, I can't give you a million examples. But here are ten mothers from the Bible who can teach us about unfailing, self-sacrificing love. We reflect on all those who have helped to shape us into followers of Christ, leading us toward eternal life.

10. Mother of the Sons of Zebedee (Matthew 20:20–28): Like all good mothers, she wanted to help her children achieve success. So she went to Jesus and asked that he grant James and John the seats at his right and left (the seats of honor) when he came into his kingdom. But Jesus transformed her request and challenged her sons to live as disciples, following him by embracing service and suffering. He called them to a life that will lead them to the cross and, ultimately, to the heavenly kingdom. Her story reminds us of what is most important in life. Authority is found not in worldly power, but in humble service. Our goal is not to gain fame and riches, but to live forever with God.

9. Hannah (1 Samuel 1:1–2:11): After many years of longing for a child with her husband, Elkanah, Hannah turned to God in prayer at his temple in Shiloh, asking him to bless her with a child. When God granted Hannah's prayer, she received that child (Samuel) as a gift and turned to God in joy-filled praise. Each child is a gift from God, to be treasured and nurtured so as to grow in God's love.

8. Naomi (The Book of Ruth): Though Naomi's sons have died at the beginning of the book, she has the unfailing loyalty of her daughter-in-law, Ruth. Though now widowed, Ruth journeys with Naomi back to her hometown of Bethlehem. Once there, Naomi provides wise counsel that helps Ruth come to the notice of Boaz, who becomes her husband. Later, Naomi adopts Ruth and Boaz's child (Obed, the father of King David) as her grandson. She reminds us that mothering is not always a matter of blood ties.

7. Elizabeth (Luke 1): Despite facing the challenge of infertility, Elizabeth lived a righteous and faithful life. She received God's promise of a child with hope and gratitude. Elizabeth welcomed her kinswoman Mary into her home and recognized the Lord in Mary's unborn child. When her own son was born, she remained faithful to God, giving him the name John as the angel had instructed Zechariah. She teaches us that mothers must persevere.

6. Eve (Genesis 2–3): Adam called her "the mother of all the living" (Genesis 3:20). She faced the greatest pain any mother can face — the loss of her child, Abel. Her pain was magnified by the fact that her son had died at his brother Cain's hand. In addition, she lived with the consequences of her own sin. She is a reminder of human frailty and resilience and of the abiding forgiveness of God.

5. Hagar (Genesis 16 and 21): Growing older with no son to inherit his land, Abraham turns to his wife Sarah's maidservant, Hagar, to conceive an heir. In due course, she bears a son, Ishmael. After Sarah has borne Isaac, Hagar and her son are forced into exile, facing incredible hardships, nearly dying of thirst and heat exhaustion as they travel through the desert. In utter despair and facing death, her concern is for her child, whom she entrusts to God's loving care.

4. Mother of the Seven Sons (2 Maccabees 7): During the reign of Antiochus Epiphanes, the Greek ruler of the conquered territory of Israel, the temple was profaned and the practice of Judaism was outlawed. Those Jews who practiced their faith were subjected to extreme persecution. The Second Book of Maccabees relates the story of an unnamed mother who witnesses the martyrdom of her children before facing the same fate. Through their suffering and pain, she supported her sons, exhorting them to courage and abiding faith.

3. Moses' Mother (Exodus 2: 1–9): In order to limit the growing power of the Hebrews, the Egyptians required that midwives kill any sons born to the Hebrew women. When the midwife spared Moses, his mother hid him from the authorities. When she could no longer hide her son, she put all her faith in God, risking everything and entrusting Moses to the waters of the Nile. She placed him in a basket concealed by the bulrushes, hoping that someone would find him and give him a chance for a life of safety. She is a model of selfless love for mothers who place their children for adoption, wanting the very best for their children.

2. The Syro-Phoenician Woman (Mark 7:24–30): This unnamed mother pleads before Jesus, asking him to heal her daughter. Jesus asks why he should heal the daughter of this foreigner, since his mission is to the children of Israel. This mother responds to Jesus' question with humility and faith, asking for what she and her daughter need. Jesus acclaims her faith and heals her daughter.

1. Mary of Nazareth (The Gospels, especially Luke 1–2, John 2 and 19, Acts 1): Mary is the perfect disciple: she says "Yes" to God, goes out of her way to aid others, and follows her Son, even to his death. As the mother of Jesus and our mother, she nurtures us in our discipleship and leads us to her Son.

ABBA, FATHER

Having looked at biblical mothers, it's time to look at fathers from the Bible who provide examples that can teach us how to love and care for those entrusted to us. These fathers share their strength and compassion, showing us the path we should follow.

10. Adam (Genesis 2–4): The founding father of all humanity, Adam faced great struggles as a parent, including the tragic murder of one son at the hands of the other. He built a life for his family, toiling with great effort to provide for their needs. Through it all, he supported his wife Eve and continued to call on the name of the Lord (Genesis 4:26).

9. Father of the Boy with a Demon (Mark 9:14–29): Though the Gospel never gives this father's name, his faith is a shining example for fathers (and others!) everywhere. After the apostles fail to heal his son, he comes to Jesus to ask for healing. Challenged by Jesus, he responds with an affirmation and prayer that should be on the lips of every Christian: "I do believe, help my unbelief!" (Mk 9:24)

8. Jacob (Genesis 27–50): Jacob's twelve sons became the founders of the twelve tribes of Israel. His family was not perfect. It was beset by jealousy, sibling rivalry, and violence. Still, Jacob loved his children deeply. His last act was to pray over his sons and ask God's blessing on them and their families. All children can benefit from their fathers' prayers.

7. Wisdom Father (Proverbs and Sirach): The books of Proverbs and Sirach feature a father giving advice to his children so that they might grow in wisdom and fear of the Lord. His advice covers practical matters, such as money and the choice of friends, as well as more spiritual matters, such as fidelity in serving the Lord. This father embraces his role as the first teacher of his children, helping to guide them on to the path of righteousness.

6. Jairus (Mark 5:21–43): A leader in the local community, Jairus humbly approaches Jesus to request healing for his seriously ill daughter. Even after he is informed of his daughter's death, he maintains his faith and hope. Jairus receives Jesus into his home and is present when Jesus raises his daughter from the dead. He models the paternal values of humility and perseverance.

5. Mordecai (Book of Esther): Mordecai welcomed Esther (Hadassah) into his family and his heart after the death of her parents, adopting her as his own daughter. Throughout her youth, and even after her marriage to King Ahasuerus, Mordecai watched out for Esther, ensuring her safety and well-being. In addition, he provided a good example by fulfilling the duties of his job with care and integrity. A good father, Mordecai encouraged Esther to follow God's call, to live faithfully in her marriage, and to intercede on behalf of her people.

4. Tobit (Book of Tobit): Living in exile in a hostile culture and struggling with his own illness, Tobit modeled just living for his son Tobiah. By example, Tobit taught his son to care for his neighbors, to obey God's law, even when difficult, and to treat his employees with justice. Through all life's challenges, Tobit also taught his son to remember to always give thanks to God.

3. Abraham (Genesis 12–25): Honored as the father in faith of Judaism, Christianity, and Islam, Abraham trusted God completely and lived in that faith. On the word of God, Abraham left his family home to travel to an unknown land. He entered into a covenant with the Lord, believing that the Lord would be faithful to his promises. His faith faced its sternest test when God asked him to offer his son Isaac as a sacrifice. Even in the face of such a challenge, his faith in God did not fail. Like all good fathers, he becomes a model of faith for his children.

2. Joseph (Matthew 1–2, Luke 1–2): Though Joseph knew that he was not the biological father of Mary's child, he accepted Jesus as his own on the message of an angel. He protected Mary and the unborn Jesus during the journey to Bethlehem and shielded them from Herod's violence by taking them to Egypt. Joseph searched for Jesus when he remained behind in Jerusalem and raised him in wisdom and grace in Nazareth. He provided for Mary and Jesus through his labor as a carpenter (Matthew 13:55). Joseph reminds us that a father's primary responsibilities are to care for his children and to raise them to know and love God.

1. God the Father (The Gospels, Romans 8:14–17): The Gospels recount Jesus' ministry, through which he revealed the Father to us. More than that, Jesus invites us to call God *Our Father* and to turn to him in prayer, trusting that our loving Father will give us all we need. We are called to enter into the close bond between Jesus and his "Abba." God our Father desires nothing more than for all his children to live in love and righteousness so as to be happy with him forever.

DADDY'S LITTLE GIRLS

In many ways, this is the most challenging of the lists. Many daughters presented in the Bible specifically as daughters (of course, every woman in the Bible is someone's *daughter) are victims. They suffer violence and abuse and may do things that are appalling to modern sensibilities. However, we cannot turn away from the challenging texts in the Bible. We must accept the view they present of the human world malformed by sin. Parents and catechists may want to use care in presenting this list to young people. Many of these stories are difficult to read and contemplate. They must spur us to promote the dignity and gifts of every human being, no matter their status or the value accorded them by their societies.*

10. Zelophehad's daughters (Numbers 27): We know almost nothing about these women, but their significance is undeniable. When their father died, questions arose about the disposition of his estate. Typically, the estate would have been divided between his sons. Zelophehad, however, had no sons. At his daughters' petition, the leaders of Israel agreed that daughters could inherit in the absence of sons. Because of their efforts, future generations of Israelite women had greater financial security.

9. Sarah (Tobit, especially chapters 3 and 7–11): The story of Sarah, the daughter of Raguel, parallels that of Tobiah, the son of Tobit. When we first meet her, she has been married to seven men but none of the marriages has been consummated. Instead, each of her husbands died on the wedding night. Taunted and bullied, even by her own servants, Sarah considers suicide. She decides against suicide because of the pain this action would cause her father, and she turns to prayer. Her marriage to Tobiah also begins with prayer. Tobiah survives the wedding night, and she returns with him to his home. They live in loving fidelity to the Lord and raise seven sons.

8. Reuel's (Jethro's) daughters (Exodus 2): Reuel, also called Jethro, was a priest in the land of Midian, in the Sinai desert region. He had seven daughters, but only one of them is named in the Bible. The daughters go to the local well, but are chased away by local shepherds. Moses, who has escaped into the desert, defends the women and helps them complete their chores. In gratitude, Jethro sends his daughters to invite Moses to stay with them. Ultimately, Moses marries the only daughter whose name we know: Zipporah.

7. Pharaoh's daughter (Exodus 2): While walking along the Nile, Pharaoh's unnamed daughter finds a baby in a basket, hidden among the reeds. Though she recognized that the child was Hebrew, and thus condemned to death, she chooses to save his life, adopting Moses as her own son. She is among the very few positive examples of Egyptians recounted in the Bible, reminding us that good can be found everywhere.

6. Lot's daughters (Genesis 19): Lot's daughters are young and unmarried, still living in their father's home when Lot extends the hospitality of his home to two strangers who are, in truth, angels of the Lord. When the local townsmen threaten the home, asking to abuse the guests, Lot offers his daughters to the unruly crowd, making them potential victims of gang rape. Fortunately for the powerless women, the offer is refused and, with their father, they escape the destruction of Sodom and Gomorrah. Later, in exile in a land where they have no prospects, the daughters get their father drunk so that he will impregnate them, giving them sons who will care for them in their old age. More than anything else, they show us the utter powerlessness experienced by many women and the desperate circumstances that they face.

5. Philip's daughters (Acts of the Apostles 21): We know very little about these four women besides the fact that they were the daughters of Philip. One of the seven original deacons, Philip is identified as an evangelist. His daughters are noted for being filled with the Holy Spirit and blessed with the gift of prophecy.

4. Dinah (Genesis 34): We see Dinah only in her victimhood. The only named daughter of Jacob, Dinah was raped by Shechem, the son of the Hivite leader. Shechem decides that he wishes to marry her. With no consideration for Dinah's feelings, her brothers decide to use the possibility of the marriage to take revenge for the assault on their sister. As a condition for the marriage, her brothers require that the men of the Hivite community accept the covenant of circumcision. While the men recover from the surgery, the brothers slaughter the Hivite community. Dinah is not mentioned again.

3. Tamar (2 Samuel 13): Tamar was the daughter of King David and the full sister of Absalom. Her half brother, Amnon, was infatuated with her and tricked her into coming to his rooms by pretending to be ill. While she was there, he raped her and then, rather than marry her (a permissible marriage at the time), he threw her out, adding humiliation to his violent assault. When David refused to take action against Amnon, Absalom killed him in revenge, forever sundering the royal family. Once again, Tamar's ultimate fate remains unrecorded.

2. Jephthah's daughter (Judges 11:29–40): The story of Jephthah's daughter is one of the most terrifying stories in the Bible. Following a great military victory, Jephthah vows that he will offer as a sacrifice the first person who greets him when he returns to his home. To his dismay, his daughter, his only child, is the first person to leave the house, greeting him with joy on account of his victory. Amazingly, she agrees to help him fulfill his vow, asking only for time to mourn before he puts her to death and offers her as a sacrifice.

1. Daughter Zion: The city of Jerusalem is often personified as Daughter Zion, the precious daughter of God. The city holds a special place in the heart of God, even when its people do not act in justice and fidelity to the covenant. A good father, God is patient, forgiving, and always faithful.

CHIPS OFF THE OLD BLOCK?

The sons of the Bible range from great heroes to great scoundrels. Yet good or bad, their lives have much to teach us.

10. Amnon (2 Samuel 13): Amnon was the firstborn son of King David. Because of his favored status, Amnon grew accustomed to having everything he wanted, regardless of the consequences. Fueled by lust, he raped his half sister Tamar and then cast her aside, heartlessly deepening her humiliation. Murdered by Absalom in revenge, Amnon proves that life without consequences is not a healthy way to raise children.

9. Absalom (2 Samuel 13–18): Amnon's half brother and the full brother of Tamar, Absalom murders Amnon and goes into exile. Though pardoned by David, his resentment toward David grows, and Absalom becomes the leader of a rebellion. In the end, the rebellion fails. Despite an order from David to protect Absalom, one of the generals kills him. Despite his son's efforts to dethrone him, David mourns his son deeply, showing the abiding love of a parent.

8. Sons of Eli (1 Samuel 2–4): Hophni and Phinehas were the sons of the priest Eli. Because Israel had a hereditary priesthood, the sons became priests when they reached adulthood. As priests, they defined corruption, stealing from the sacrifices and seducing the women who served there. To their father's despair, they had little desire to aid the faithful in authentic worship. Having lost God's favor, they died in a battle against the Philistines.

7. The Man Born Blind (John 9): Jesus comes across an unnamed man who was born blind, sitting along the roadside. Though it was the Sabbath, Jesus healed him by making mud and spreading it over his eyes. When the man washed the mud away, his sight was restored. This violation of the Sabbath attracted the attention of the religious leaders who interrogated the man and his parents. Fearing the leaders and the possibility of expulsion from the synagogue, his parents would say only that he had been born blind and that they did not know how he had been healed. Despite his parents' fear, this man refuses to change his story and he worships Jesus as the Messiah.

6. Samson (Judges 13–16): Samson was the son of Manoah and his wife. His birth, after years of infertility, was announced by an angel's message. In addition to the announcement, the angel gave instructions for raising the child. Manoah and his wife took these instructions seriously, even asking God to send the angel again to provide more assistance. God had designated Samson for a special mission, using his strength to help the Israelites break the domination of the Philistines. Though Samson was not always a model of good behavior, in the end, his parents' instruction prevailed and he remained faithful to God.

5. Judas Maccabeus (1 and 2 Maccabees): The son of Mattathias, a faithful follower of the covenant, Judas led his brothers in a revolt against the Seleucid kings who controlled the land of Israel and persecuted the practice of the Jewish faith. Judas's nickname, Maccabeus, means "the hammer," a sign of his skill in military endeavors. He was successful in cleansing and rededicating the Temple in Jerusalem, an event celebrated on the Jewish feast of Hanukkah. Judas donated money to provide for expiatory sacrifices for his soldiers who had died in battle, believing that they would be raised from the dead. When he died in battle, the people of Israel mourned his death.

4. The Holy Innocents (Matthew 2): When the magi visited Herod to seek the newborn king of the Jews, they aroused his jealousy and fear. Though he asked the magi to report back to him with the child's identity, the magi went home by a different route, leaving Herod without the information. Determined to eliminate any threats to his throne, Herod decreed that all boys in Bethlehem under the age of two should die. The names of these murdered sons have not been recorded, but echoes of their parents' grief resound in all the places of the world where children die before their time due to illness and violence.

3. Isaac (Genesis 21–22): Isaac was the long-awaited and much-beloved son of Abraham and Sarah. The Lord had promised Abraham that, through Isaac, he would have many descendants. Yet, while Isaac was still young, the Lord commanded Abraham to offer him as a sacrifice. When Abraham showed himself willing to follow the Lord's command, an angel stopped his hand. Isaac lived and became the second of the three great patriarchs. He learned from his father the value of abiding faith in the one true God.

2. Tobiah (Book of Tobit): Tobiah is the son of Tobit and Anna. His parents raise him to keep to the covenant and to care for his neighbors. Tobit even counsels him about the need to pay his workers fairly. Tobiah learns these lessons well and becomes a man of justice and integrity who turns regularly to the Lord in prayer.

1. Jesus (Gospels): Jesus is the beloved only-begotten Son of the Father. He undertook the ministry set forth by his Father and conformed his will completely to that of his Father. All Christians are called to conform themselves to Christ, through him becoming faithful sons and daughters of the one we may call "our Father."

SIBLING RIVALRY

Brothers and sisters can be the best of friends or the most bitter of enemies. The siblings in the Bible show us these extremes, testifying to the complexity of human behavior.

10. Jacob's Sons (Genesis 29–50): Jacob's twelve sons, the namesakes of the twelve tribes of Israel, had four different mothers (not unusual in a world where polygamy and concubinage were commonly accepted). The brothers, jealous of Joseph who was Jacob's favorite, considered killing him but decide to sell him into slavery instead. Yet the Bible offers some proof of the love that abided among these brothers. Reuben and Judah interceded to save Joseph's life. The brothers banded together to avenge Dinah's rape. Joseph used his power in Egypt to save and reunite his family. No matter their challenges, the bonds of family run deep.

9. Shem, Ham, and Japheth (Genesis 6–9): Noah's sons, along with their wives, were saved in the ark from the ravages of the flood. The sons share in God's covenant with their father — the promise that God will never again destroy all life on earth. After leaving the ark, Ham embarrassed his father Noah, to his brothers' dismay. Because of Ham's lack of respect, Noah cursed him to be his brother's slave. In the nineteenth century, the biblical passage regarding the curse was used by some people to justify the enslavement of African Americans.

8. Cain and Abel (Genesis 4): Well, given that it culminated in the first recorded murder, this sibling relationship was clearly dysfunctional! The source of the conflict is clear: Cain became jealous because God preferred Abel's sacrifice. Cain blamed Abel and murdered him. When God came to Cain in search of Abel, Cain asked the immortal question, "Am I my brother's keeper?" (Genesis 4:9). For a person of faith, the answer must be yes.

7. Jonathan and Milcah (1 Samuel 14–2 Samuel 6): Of all Saul's children, Jonathan and Milcah are closest to David. Milcah becomes David's wife and Jonathan is David's closest friend. Despite her marriage, Milcah's loyalties seem to remain with her father. Jonathan, on the other hand, acts as an intermediary between David and his father. Though family ties are important, a truly loving family is open to others.

6. Jacob and Esau (Genesis 25, 27, and 33): Jacob and Esau, though twins, are quite different personalities. Esau, the elder and the favorite of his father Isaac, is the rugged outdoorsman. Jacob is his mother Rebekah's favorite and more of a homebody. Though Esau is the firstborn son, Jacob buys his birthright in exchange for some bread and stew. Jacob later tricks his elderly father so that Isaac grants him the special blessing intended for Esau. Despite the conflicts of their early years, Jacob and Esau reconcile later in life, as each man has made his own way into adulthood. We must find the courage to move past old hurts and find new paths of reconciliation.

5. The Seven Sons of a Faith-Filled Mother (2 Maccabees 7): These brothers are never named, yet the story of their martyrdom is among the most memorable in the Bible. Though the Hellenists had outlawed the practice of Judaism, these brothers, along with their exceptionally brave mother, remained faithful to the covenant. Brought before the authorities, they were tortured harshly and executed in turn. Despite the emotional and physical pain they suffered, the brothers refused to renounce their faith. Encouraging each other and supported by their mother, these brothers faced death together, confident that they would be together again in the Kingdom of heaven.

4. James and John (Gospels): The sons of Zebedee, James and John are also called the sons of thunder. As the nickname indicates, they were a bit hot-headed and ambitious. They were always eager to ensure their status. Indeed, they were two of the three Apostles chosen to witness the raising of Jairus's daughter, the Transfiguration, and the agony in the Garden of Gethsemane. They wanted to ensure that no one but the Twelve preached the Gospel and that they would have the seats of honor when Jesus began his reign. Jesus never discounted their enthusiasm. He just helped them to see that following him is not about power and status, but service and sacrifice.

3. Simon Peter and Andrew (Gospels): Andrew gave Simon Peter the greatest gift a brother can give — he introduced him to Jesus (cf. John 1). The brothers were called to be among the Twelve Apostles. They travelled with Jesus throughout his public ministry and preached the Gospel throughout the known world after Pentecost.

2. Moses, Miriam, Aaron (Exodus): These siblings work together closely to help liberate the Israelites from slavery in Egypt. Moses was commissioned by God to lead the people out of Egypt, but Aaron acted as his spokesman before

Pharaoh. After the exodus from Egypt, Aaron and his sons became the first priests, responsible for the ritual worship of the community. Miriam watched over the baby Moses, protecting him while he was hidden on the banks of the Nile. Later, she led the community in a song of praise following the crossing of the Red Sea. Though they struggled with jealousy from time to time, the bonds of love between these three helped lead the people of Israel to the Promised Land.

1. Mary, Martha, Lazarus (Luke 10 and John 11–12): The closeness of these siblings is rivaled only by their close relationship with Jesus. Jesus stayed in their home during his travels. Jesus raised Lazarus from the dead, though he must have known that such a sign would inflame his enemies. Martha made a clear profession of faith in Jesus as the Messiah. Mary braved scorn and custom to anoint Jesus' feet before his passion. Though they have typical sibling quarrels about doing the chores, the deep love these siblings share is unmistakable. And they teach us an important lesson: The closer they become to Christ, the closer they become to each other.

AH, GLORIOUS YOUTH

Let's look at ten young people in the Bible who are models for all the faithful, no matter how old we are! May those who have gone before us in faith serve as inspirations to live our faith well from the first days of our lives to the last.

10. Timothy (Acts of the Apostles, 1 and 2 Timothy): Paul cautioned his fellow missionary Timothy against letting anyone discount his message because of his youth. Despite his youth, Timothy traveled around the Roman Empire preaching the Gospel of Jesus Christ with courage and conviction. All the baptized, regardless of age, are called to proclaim Christ in their words and actions.

9. Joshua (Exodus, Deuteronomy, Joshua): Though Joshua is better known for his later leadership of the Israelite community (and for a certain battle at Jericho), we first see him as Moses' assistant. He spent his earliest years as an apprentice to Moses, learning from him and growing in his relationship to the Lord. He reminds us of the importance of following reliable spiritual teachers who will help us grow in faith.

8. Jeremiah (Jeremiah): Jeremiah's first recorded words are a complaint that he's too young to serve as God's prophet. God tells him in no uncertain terms that he has an important role to play, regardless of his age. He simply needs to repeat what God tells him to say. Jeremiah's prophetic mission brought him great hardship, but he called the people to authentic faith and comforted them in exile.

7. Rebekah (Genesis): We first see Rebekah when her father asks her if she will leave her family and her home to marry Isaac. Despite her youth and the anxiety she must have felt, she immediately agreed to go. She became one of the great matriarchs of the Jewish people. God may call us to set out on unknown paths that may be frightening, but he will always be with us to care for us on the way.

6. Abel (Genesis 4): Abel's story is recounted in just a few short verses, but those verses teach an important lesson. Abel's sacrifice is pure and heartfelt. He does not give God what he has left over, but gives to God first, the very best he has. When we give our best to God, holding nothing back, God will never leave us wanting.

5. Solomon (1 Kings): Solomon became the King of Israel while still a young man. God invited him to ask for any gift he desired. Instead of asking for material possessions or worldly power, Solomon asked for wisdom so that he would be a good ruler. In response, God blessed him with abundant wisdom. Though he later wandered away from his relationship with God, in his youth, Solomon could teach us a lot about choosing gifts of true and lasting value.

4. Samuel (1 Samuel): Samuel's mother Hannah dedicated him to service in the temple while he was still a child. One night, as Samuel was falling asleep, he heard God calling him. Though at first he did not recognize the Lord's voice, with the counsel of the wise older priest Eli, Samuel learned to listen to the Lord.

3. Daniel (Daniel): As a youth, Daniel was brought into the court of the King of Babylon to be trained for royal service. Despite the temptation to seek power and to follow the crowd, he remained true to his faith and, ultimately, became a prophet, speaking God's truth to the people.

2. Mary (Luke 1): Scripture does not record Mary's childhood. We first see her receiving the angel's message that God has chosen her to bear his Son. Though she did not understand the angel's message and she had to be more than a little bit afraid, she accepted God's plan for her and answered "Yes" to his call.

1. Jesus in the Temple (Luke 2): Few incidents of Jesus' early life in Nazareth are recounted in Scripture. But Luke tells of a Passover trip to Jerusalem when Jesus was only twelve. When his parents headed home, Jesus remained behind in Jerusalem. His parents found him three days later, sitting in the temple, talking with the elders and teachers. Jesus went home and was obedient to his parents, "growing in wisdom and age and favor" (Luke 2:52). Jesus models for us the desire we should have to learn more about our faith and to live that faith in love and obedience.

LOOKING FOR LOVE

Check out these top ten love stories that have withstood the test of time and take some time to think about the love story you could be writing today as you live these examples in your own married life.

10. Tobiah and Sarah (Tobit 7–8): A classic story of love at first sight, this couple overcame personal tragedy to establish a long-lasting relationship founded on prayer.

9. The Woman of Worth and Her (Unnamed) Husband (Proverbs 31:10–31): A lovely poem praising a woman who can do it all! She and her husband have a wonderful partnership, using their gifts to the benefit of their family and community.

8. Hosea and Gomer (Hosea 1–3): Though their marriage was fraught with infidelity and difficulties, their love story speaks to the healing power of forgiveness and its necessity in any loving relationship.

7. Abraham and Sarah (Genesis 12–23): No one can say that Abraham and Sarah had it easy. They faced a long move away from family, jealousy, and the challenge of infertility, yet their love was the foundation of a new people, living in covenant with the one true God.

6. Moses and Zipporah (Exodus 2, 4, and 18, and Numbers 12): While in exile from Egypt, Moses married Zipporah, the daughter of the Midianite priest, Jethro. Though Moses was criticized for taking a foreign wife, Zipporah showed great respect for her husband's faith and his mission.

5. Zechariah and Elizabeth (Luke 1–2): These parents of John the Baptist provide a model of lifelong fidelity and righteousness, living their marital love in the heart of their close-knit faith community.

4. Jacob and Rachel (Genesis 29–30): Tricked into marrying her older sister, Jacob worked for Rachel's father an additional seven years to earn her hand in marriage. Jacob and Rachel remind us that true love always requires effort and sacrifice.

3. The Bride and Groom in the Song of Songs (Song of Songs 1–8): This young couple reminds us that passion is not a modern invention! After all, who could resist hearing their beloved say, "You ravished my heart with one glance of your eyes" (Song of Songs 4:9)? Their effusive love for each other speaks to the beauty of loving desire at the heart of a marriage.

2. Joseph and Mary (Matthew 1–2, Luke 1–2): Though this marriage definitely faced difficulties, even before it started, Joseph and Mary's faith in each other and, even more, in God, allowed them to face each hardship and create a loving family to nurture God's own Son.

1. God and His People: At its heart, the entire Bible is the story of the love God has for the people he created in his own image and likeness. From the Old Testament images of Israel as the Bride of the Lord to the New Testament images of the Church as the Bride of Christ, God's love remains constant and unfailing. Though we often reject his love,

God never withdraws, never walks away, even sending his only-begotten Son to offer the gift of salvation and everlasting life! And that gift is still offered to us today!

THANK YOU FOR BEING A FRIEND

The books of Scripture show us friendship in its many forms. Friends can be good influences or bad, and the Bible shows us both. It even gives advice on how to tell the difference!

10. Paul and Luke (Acts 16 and 20; 2 Timothy 4): From the evidence we have in the Acts of the Apostles and the Second Letter to Timothy, it seems that Luke traveled with Paul on some of his missionary journeys, recording Paul's teaching and providing a written account of events. Paul considered him a faithful companion, and Luke returned the favor, speaking highly of Paul's eloquent preaching.

9. Esther and Hegai (Esther 2): Esther and Hegai show a different type of friendship: that between mentor and protégé. Esther was the outsider who entered the king's harem in a competition to become the new queen. As head eunuch, Hegai was responsible for all the "contestants." Esther willingly accepted his advice, and her efforts were successful. A mentor is a good friend who can help you develop and use your gifts to the fullest.

8. Amnon and Jonadab (2 Samuel 13): Amnon and Jonadab show the negative side of friendship. Rather than encouraging virtuous living and good choices, Jonadab encouraged Amnon to follow his passions and assault Tamar. Far from counseling against such a sinful action, Jonadab actually facilitated the violence. A bad friend is a pathway to evil.

7. Faithful Friend (Sirach): The Book of Sirach (the Wisdom of Ben Sira) offers a primer on friendship, explaining how to choose friends, how to tell good friends from bad ones, and the qualities a good friend will bring to the relationship. Good friends will lead you to Wisdom and to a deeper relationship with God.

6. Job, Bildad, Zophar, and Eliphaz (Job 2–31): Most of the Book of Job consists of a series of speeches and replies between Job and his three friends. When his friends heard of Job's misfortunes, they undertook journeys to visit Job and to offer him their sympathy. For seven days and seven nights, they sit with him in the dust, sharing his suffering. Their speeches are earnest, if misguided, attempts to help Job make sense of his predicament.

5. Tobiah and Raphael (Tobit 5–12): Tobit hires the disguised angel Raphael to travel with his son Tobiah on a business trip to distant relatives. The nature of the trip requires a faithful companion since, on the return journey, the travelers would be carrying a substantial sum of money. Tobiah and Raphael formed a good partnership. Tobiah shared his feelings and challenges and Raphael offered helpful advice. Once the trip was completed, Raphael revealed his angelic nature and returned to heaven. And we can't forget man's best friend! Tobiah's dog faithfully followed Tobiah and Raphael on their way.

4. Paul and Barnabas (Acts 9, 12–14): In the days following Paul's conversion, Christians treated him with suspicion — unsurprising given that Paul's mission in life was the persecution of Christians. However, once Paul returned to Jerusalem, Barnabas took Paul's part and helped him integrate into the Church community. Later, Paul and Barnabas journeyed together, preaching the Gospel throughout Asia Minor. Unfortunately, their friendship and joint ministry ended after a sharp disagreement about who should be part of a mission trip.

3. Judith and Her Maid (Judith 8–16): Throughout Judith's brave efforts to end the siege on her town, she had one companion — her maid. They worked together to spring the trap on Holofernes and his army. Judith couldn't have done it alone, and both faced grave danger in carrying out the plan. As a reward, Judith gave her maid freedom. Though their statuses were not equal, they respected each other and worked well together.

2. David and Jonathan (1 Samuel 18 and 20, 2 Samuel 1): David and Jonathan shared the closest friendship recorded in Scripture. Closer than family, they served Jonathan's father, King Saul, together. Though David took Jonathan's place as the heir to the throne, Jonathan doesn't seem to have been jealous. He defended David, protecting him from Saul's tempers. David gave Jonathan his complete trust and mourned his death deeply. David had brothers and wives and children, but no relationship closer than his friendship with Jonathan.

1. Jesus and the Beloved Disciple (John, especially chapters 13 and 19–21): The Beloved Disciple shares a close friendship with Jesus. He reclines next to Jesus at the Last Supper. (In Jesus' time, following the Roman custom, important meals were eaten lying on couches.) The Beloved Disciple stays with Jesus at the foot of the cross and receives

Mary into his care. On the Sea of Tiberius after the Resurrection, he is the first to recognize Jesus. This disciple is never named, perhaps as a reminder that we should all strive to develop such a close relationship with Jesus.

HOLDING OUT FOR SOME HEROES

These heroes in the Bible don't have superpowers, but they do have great courage and faith. They faced grave challenges or took actions that greatly benefitted others. If you're holding out for a hero, here are (more than) ten.

10. Jael (Judges 4–5): Jael was not a warrior, but she used guile to kill Sisera, a great general who led a Canaanite army against the Israelites. She risked her family's alliances and her own safety to ensure that this skilled general would not return to battle the people of Israel.

9. Hezekiah (2 Kings 18–20; 2 Chronicles 29–32; Isaiah 36–38): Hezekiah was a King of Judah. He had a great military triumph when the Assyrian siege of Jerusalem was ended by the sudden death of a significant portion of the Assyrian forces (one of history's great mysteries). Even more importantly, Hezekiah was faithful to the Lord, keeping the covenant and putting an end to the worship of other gods.

8. Cyrus and Darius (Ezra): Cyrus and Darius were Persian kings who released the Israelites from exile in Babylon, allowing them to return to Jerusalem and rebuild the Temple. They showed kindness and mercy to their captives, the hallmarks of heroic rulers.

7. Josiah (2 Kings 22–23; 2 Chronicles 34–35): Josiah became King of Judah when he was only eight years old. At that time, Israel had fallen away from keeping the covenant. When Josiah was eighteen, his officials found a copy of the Law of Moses tucked away in a storeroom. Josiah read the Law and asked the people to recommit to the covenant. Wanting what was best for his people, he instituted religious reforms to purge pagan practices and restore worship in the Temple.

6. Gideon (Judges 6–7): God called Gideon to be a judge, ruling the Hebrew people once they settled in the Promised Land. In Gideon's time, the Israelites faced a serious threat from the people of Midian. Before Gideon defeated Midian in battle, he destroyed the altar of Baal set up in Israel, instead building an altar of sacrifice to the Lord. Gideon understood that Israel's fortunes as a nation depended on their fidelity to the Lord, worshipping only the one true God.

5. Esther (Book of Esther): Though Jewish, Esther was the queen consort of the Persian king, rising to that position because of her beauty. However, when the Jewish people were threatened with extermination by the evil minister Haman, Esther put her own life on the line to plead their case with her husband. She risked her own safety and position for those in need, making her a true hero.

4. Judith (Book of Judith): A pious widow, Judith abandoned her widow's weeds and her seclusion to save her town from a siege. She entered the enemy camp by pretending to be a refugee from the besieged city and she used her great beauty to capture the attention of the general, Holofernes. She turned his plan to seduce her against him and killed him instead. The death of their general forced the besieging army's retreat, saving the city. Judith shunned the resulting fame and returned to her quiet life of religious devotion.

3. Shadrach, Meshach, and Abednego (Daniel 3): These three young men were Jewish exiles in Babylon, selected for training to serve the Babylonian king. Despite their exposure to the Babylonian royal court, they remained faithful to the covenant, even when they were threatened with death. Because of their faith, they were sentenced to death in a furnace. However, God protected them, and they were able to walk around the furnace without harm. Their faith and God's power in saving them won the king's respect.

2. David (1 and 2 Samuel): David began his military career with the defeat of the Philistine giant Goliath and then entered the service of King Saul. David continued to have military success, and God chose him to succeed Saul as King of Israel. David became the greatest king Israel ever knew. He established the capital in Jerusalem and kept the people faithful to the covenant. God promised him that his kingdom would continue. Through Jesus, the son of David, that promise was fulfilled.

1. Eleazar (2 Maccabees 6:18–31): Eleazar was a well-respected scribe during the time of great religious persecution under Antiochus Epiphanes. As part of the persecution, Jews were forced to eat pork in violation of the Law of Moses. Those who refused to eat were tortured and executed. Because Eleazar was elderly and popular, his persecutors offered to let him fake the test, replacing the pork with meat that he could eat. But Eleazar refused this concession, pointing out that seeing him appear to violate the law would be a scandal to faithful Jews, especially the young. He accepted martyrdom rather than betray the Law and lead others astray. His courage in the face of ridicule and torture makes him one of Scripture's greatest heroes.

UNSUNG HEROES

Not all the heroes in the Bible are well known. The marks of a hero are courage, compassion, and fidelity, not fame. These unsung heroes left their marks on biblical history, even if we don't recognize their names today.

10. Jonathan (1 Maccabees 10–13): Jonathan succeeded Judas Maccabeus as the leader of the revolt against Antiochus Epiphanes. In addition to his military successes, he gave a great deal of attention to religious fidelity. He served as high priest of the Temple in Jerusalem and promoted fidelity to the covenant.

9. Ebed-melech (Jeremiah 38): Ebed-melech, though an Ethiopian, served as an official of the King of Judah during the time when Jeremiah was prophesying. Jeremiah's preaching aroused much opposition, and his opponents convinced the king to throw Jeremiah into an empty cistern where he was likely to die of starvation. Ebed-melech went to the king and successfully pleaded for Jeremiah's life, seeing that he was rescued from the cistern so he could continue his preaching.

8. Ezra (Ezra, Nehemiah): Ezra was a priest and scribe, knowledgeable about the Law and faithful to the Lord. He was part of the group of Israelites who, with the permission of King Cyrus, returned to Judah from exile in Babylon. Ezra was pivotal in re-establishing the Jewish community after the lengthy exile. He encouraged the people to be faithful to the Law and to base their community on their covenant with the Lord.

7. Apollos (Acts 18:24–25): Apollos was well known for his preaching skill and his knowledge of Scripture. Though he had received only the baptism of John, he did know of Jesus. Priscilla and Aquila gave him further instruction about Jesus and Christian living. Following this instruction, Apollos became a great evangelist, preaching Jesus Christ and using Scripture to prove that Jesus was the Messiah.

6. Gamaliel (Acts 5:17–42): Gamaliel was a Pharisee and a great teacher of Judaism. Paul was one of his students. Gamaliel showed his wisdom when the Apostles were brought before the Sanhedrin, charged with preaching about Christ. Many members of the Sanhedrin wanted to punish the Apostles for continuing to preach even after being ordered to stop. Gamaliel wisely recalled that similar movements had occurred in the past, but all ran out of steam once their leaders died. He reasoned that if the "Jesus movement" was of human origin, it would go the way of the others. However, if it was of God, the Sanhedrin could not stop it. Gamaliel's argument won the day, and the Apostles were released after being flogged.

5. Caleb (Numbers 13–14; Ben Sira 46:7–10): Caleb, a member of the tribe of Judah, was one of the twelve scouts sent by Moses to explore the Promised Land in advance of the Israelites' approach. Most of the scouts counseled against entering the land of Canaan, opining that the people living there were too strong for the Israelites to defeat them. Only Caleb maintained that the Israelites could defeat the

Canaanites and take possession of the land, believing in the promise of the Lord.

4. Simeon and Anna (Luke 2:22–38): We see Simeon and Anna only briefly. Both were present in the Temple when Joseph and Mary bring Jesus to the Temple for the purification rites. Simeon was faithful to the covenant and had been told by God that he would not die until he had seen the Messiah. Called to the Temple by the Spirit, Simeon saw the baby Jesus and recognized that the Messiah had come. He commended himself to God and blessed Mary and Joseph. Anna was a devout widow who spent the days of her widowhood in prayer in the Temple. She too recognized Jesus, and she spoke about him to all she encountered. These devout elderly Jews were among the first people to proclaim Jesus.

3. Job (Job): Job was a wealthy Jewish man noted for his devotion to the Lord. When Satan claimed that Job was devoted to God only because his life has been easy and successful, God gave Satan permission to test Job. Satan deprived Job of his wealth, his children, and even his own health. In spite of this hardship, Job refused to curse God. In a culture where illness and hardship were considered penalties for sin, Job's friends questioned what Job might have done to deserve such punishment. Though Job fell into despair, even wishing that he had never been born, he did not curse God, and he ultimately accepted that he can never fathom the depths of God's mind. As a reward for his faithfulness, God restored Job's prosperity and gave him more children to carry on his family name.

2. Thomas (John 11:1–16; 20:19–29): Poor Thomas, consigned to history as "Doubting Thomas," known only for his worst moment. In truth, the portrait of Thomas in the Gospel of John shows a man of uncommon courage. When Jesus is called to Bethany to tend to the dying Lazarus, the Apostles counsel against the trip because the people in the region of Bethany had wanted to stone Jesus during his last visit. Thomas is the Apostle who suggested that they go with Jesus to Bethany, even if it means that they will die with Jesus. Similarly, Thomas missed the appearance of Jesus on the night of the Resurrection because he was not with the other disciples. The disciples were in hiding behind locked doors, afraid that they might share Jesus' fate. Thomas alone was out and about, not hiding in fear. And when he comes face to face with Jesus, Thomas responds with humility and adoration. So much more than a doubter!

1. Joseph of Arimathea (Matthew 27:57–61; Mark 15:42–47; Luke 23:50–56; John 19:38–42): Joseph of Arimathea was a respected Jewish official but, unlike most of the council, he was not part of the plot to kill Jesus. After Jesus' death, Joseph went to Pilate to ask for Jesus' body. Often, crucified bodies were left for scavengers, an abomination to the Jews. Asking for the body of an executed criminal took courage. To this courage, Joseph added compassion, wrapping the dead body of Jesus in a shroud and giving him a place in a tomb hewn from stone, a far better tomb than a poor itinerant preacher could have afforded on his own. In spite of his despair at Jesus' death, Joseph did what he could to show his abiding love and respect.

HOLY WOMEN WITH ATTITUDE

We often think of holy people, especially holy women, as meek, quiet, and reserved. While that may be true in some cases, here are ten biblical women with the courage of their convictions. These women were tough enough to take on the enemies of their people and the scorn of society and to accept enormous challenges. These holy women with attitude have something to teach all of us about being strong in faith and standing up for justice and for our beliefs.

10. Jael (Judges 4:17–22): Acting by subterfuge, luring him to her tent with the opportunity for food and rest, Jael killed Sisera, a Canaanite general who was besieging the people of Israel. Though the Israelite forces were on his trail, it is Jael, the wife of a nomad, who defeated this great warrior. This woman, though she had little power on her own, managed to save the people of Israel from conquest and won for herself the acclaim of the people.

9. Anointing woman (Matthew 26:6–13; Mark 14:3–9; Luke 7:36–50; John 12:1–8): Each Gospel recounts an incident in which a woman anoints Jesus' feet with precious oil. Only John's Gospel gives the woman a name — Mary of Bethany, the sister of Martha and Lazarus. Luke's Gospel identifies the woman as a notorious sinner. We do not know if the Gospels recount different anointings by different women or if the same incident has been related in different ways. In either case, we must recognize the courage it took for this woman to approach the Teacher, Jesus, during a dinner gathering; the humility it took for her to anoint his feet; and, the compassion and love with which Jesus responds to her. Mark's Gospel promises that she and her loving care will be remembered always, wherever the good news is proclaimed.

8. Deborah (Judges 4–5): Before Saul became the first king of Israel, the people were ruled by a series of judges who maintained order and resolved disputes. Some judges were good, leading the people in fidelity to the covenant, making just decisions, and protecting the Israelites from their enemies. Other judges were poor leaders, falling away from the worship of the one true God. One of the good judges was a woman named Deborah. Also acknowledged as a prophet, she was faithful to the Lord. She called forth a general to lead the army against the Canaanites. Deborah's song of praise to the Lord after the battle is one of the first hymns recorded in the Bible.

7. Ruth (Book of Ruth): A Moabite by birth, Ruth was not part of the people of Israel, though her husband was an Israelite. After his untimely death, she chose to stay with her mother-in-law Naomi, accompanying her to her ancestral home in Bethlehem. Though an outsider, Ruth risked isolation and loneliness to care for Naomi. At Naomi's instruction, she went into the fields to gather the crops left by the reapers (a privilege of widows). Her faithfulness to her mother-in-law impressed the owner of the field, Boaz, who offered her his protection. Later, taking Naomi's advice once again, Ruth came to Boaz after the harvest, seeking his continued care. In time, Boaz married Ruth, and their great grandson was Israel's greatest king, David. Because of her compassion and courage, this outsider takes her place in the genealogy of the Christ.

6. Tamar (Genesis 38): Tamar married the eldest son of Judah, one of Jacob's twelve sons. When her husband died, she married his next oldest brother. Tamar's second husband refused to give her the child that would provide for her future and continue his brother's line. As a result, God struck him down. Having lost two sons who were married to Tamar, Judah hesitated to marry her to his remaining son. Deprived of her rights, Tamar took matters into her own hands, disguising herself as a prostitute and meeting Judah by the side of the road. When her pregnancy was discovered and she was threatened with punishment, she turned the tables on Judah. He recognized that she had acted in pursuit of justice. Tamar, who risked her life to fight for her rights, is part of Jesus' family history as recounted by Matthew (1:1–18).

5. Rahab (Joshua 2, 6:22–25): Rahab is identified as a prostitute in the city of Jericho. When the Israelites sent spies into Jericho to prepare for the advance of the whole people, Rahab risked herself and her family to hide the spies from the authorities. In exchange, the spies promised to protect her family in the upcoming battle. The Israelites kept their word and Rahab's family were the only Jericho residents to survive the battle. Rahab married into the Israelite community and joined the list of women with attitude in Jesus' genealogy.

4. Esther (Book of Esther): Esther got a rough start in life. She was a Jewish orphan in exile in Persia. Adopted by Mordecai, she won a rather scandalous contest to become the queen. As queen, she became aware of a plot to kill all the

Jews. After prayer and fasting, she risked her life to petition the king to allow the Jews to defend themselves. Through her intervention, the Jewish community survived and their opponents were punished. Her achievements are celebrated to this day in the festival of Purim.

3. Mary Magdalene (Gospels, especially Matthew 28, Mark 16, Luke 24, John 20): Mary Magdalene may be one of the most misrepresented people in the Bible. No biblical evidence identifies her as either a repentant prostitute or as the leader of the early Christian community. Despite the stories (and paintings and films) about her, what the Bible actually says about her qualifies her as a holy woman with attitude. She was part of a group of women who followed Jesus from Galilee, supporting his ministry. The Gospels report that she is one of the few people with the courage to stand at the foot of Jesus' cross. After Jesus' death, she went to his tomb early Sunday morning, only to discover that he was risen. She was charged with sharing this good news with the Apostles. This faithful disciple, the Apostle to the Apostles, reminds us to stay close to Christ always and to proclaim the good news to all we meet.

2. Judith (Book of Judith): Judith was a devout widow in a small Jewish town besieged by enemy forces. As the siege took its toll on her community, Judith decided to do what she could to break the siege. Putting off her widow's garb and dressing to impress, she insinuated herself into the enemy camp, seeking protection for herself and her maid. Stunned by her beauty, the General Holofernes treated her as an honored guest, clearly hoping to seduce her. Though she led Holofernes to believe he would be successful, Judith remained faithful to the covenant, even refusing food from the general's table. In the end, Judith used Holofernes' lust to defeat him, beheading him while he was in a drunken sleep. Judith returned to her people and, when the besieged Israelites displayed Holofernes' head to the enemy soldiers, the army retreated. Having saved her people from the siege, Judith rejected offers of marriage and riches, returning to her quiet and faith-filled life.

1. Mary (Gospels, especially Luke 1–2, and Acts 1): Though Mary may not have killed enemy generals or faced off against kings, she had great courage. She accepted the scandal and scorn of conceiving Jesus though she was not yet married. In the early days of her pregnancy, she traveled to visit her kinswoman Elizabeth to support her in her pregnancy. In the last days of her pregnancy, she traveled to Bethlehem where Jesus was born. She left family and friends behind to go to Egypt so she could protect Jesus. She nurtured and supported Jesus through his youth and public ministry, following him even to the foot of the cross. After the Ascension, she prayed with the Apostles, waiting for the descent of the Holy Spirit. Such faithfulness through sorrow and joy, through love and fear, is the essence of holiness with an attitude!

UNDERDOGS

Everyone loves an underdog, and God is no exception. The Bible includes many stories of God favoring the weak, the poor, and the powerless. And these underdogs have done great things.

10. Abigail (1 Samuel 25): Abigail was the wife of a rude, ignorant, and abusive man named Nabal. His name means "fool," and he was well-named. Nabal even picked a fight with David, one that assured that he and his men would meet an untimely end. Without her husband's knowledge, Abigail calmed David's temper and saved her household. This powerless, abused wife resolved a dangerous situation. After her husband died of an apparent heart attack, David proposed to Abigail, and she became a wife of the king.

9. Gideon (Judges 6): Gideon is best known as a great judge who led the Israelites in battle against the forces of Midian, but he came from much more humble beginnings. When the angel informed Gideon of God's plan for him to lead, Gideon demurred because he was a lowly member of a lowly household. God discounted status in society and chose the man he wanted, making Gideon a great leader.

8. Zacchaeus (Luke 19:1–10): Zacchaeus has two strikes against him. First, he was a tax collector, regarded by his community as a corrupt collaborator and a public sinner. Second, he was short. When Jesus came to visit Jericho, where Zacchaeus lived, Zacchaeus wanted to see Jesus. Being too short to see over the crowds, Zacchaeus climbed a tree to get a bird's-eye view. Jesus raised eyebrows by calling Zacchaeus out of the tree and eating dinner at his home. The encounter ended with Zacchaeus promising to live his life and conduct his business with generosity and integrity.

7. Jacob (Genesis 27): Jacob was the younger son. By rights, his brother, Esau, should have inherited the bulk of their father Isaac's estate. But Jacob and his mother, Rebekah, tricked Isaac into giving Jacob the blessing intended for the firstborn. Jacob was not only the younger son; he was not the strong, rugged outdoorsman and skilled hunter that his brother was. Yet, in the end, he became one of the great patriarchs and his twelve sons founded the twelve tribes of Israel.

6. The Woman at the Well (John 4): This unnamed woman was a Samaritan, immediately making her an outsider to the Jews. In addition, she seems to have had a somewhat checkered past. By the time she encountered Jesus at the well, she had already had five husbands, and she was auditioning number six. Despite her outsider status, Jesus approached her, engaged her in conversation, and even revealed that he was the Messiah. Her witness to Jesus brought her friends and neighbors to hear his preaching and many came to believe in Jesus.

5. Leah (Genesis 29): Leah was Jacob's unloved wife. Jacob was desperately in love with Rachel, Leah's younger sister. Their father, Laban, tricked Jacob into marrying Leah before he would permit marriage to Rachel. It's impossible to imagine how difficult Leah's life must have been, always knowing that she was loved less than her younger sister, always a second thought in her own home. But God looked on Leah with kindness, and she became the mother of six sons and a daughter. Half of the tribes of Israel trace their ancestry through Leah, and Israel's two greatest sons are her progeny: King David and Jesus.

4. The Poor Widow (Mark 12:41–44): Poor widows are certainly underdogs. They have no family for protection, and they often lack even the basic necessities of life. One day, while Jesus was teaching in the Temple, he saw a poor widow come to make her contribution to the Temple treasury. Her contribution was very small, far less than the contributions made by others. Yet Jesus called attention to her generosity, noting that she gave from her want rather than from her abundance. Despite her underdog status, her generosity and trust are a model for us all.

3. The Good Thief (Luke 23:39–43): Though he is popularly called "The Good Thief" or Dismas, we know neither his criminal offense nor his name. It's tough to think of a bigger underdog than a convicted criminal in the process of being executed for his crimes. Yet the Good Thief has saved his best moment for last. In his final hours, he accepts responsibility for his own failings and asks Jesus to remember him. Jesus promises the thief that he will enter Paradise.

2. Joseph (Genesis 37–50): Though Joseph was Jacob's favorite son, his brothers sold him into slavery in Egypt. Despite initial success in Egypt, he ended up in jail. Though a prisoner, his skill at interpreting dreams allowed him to rise in status, eventually becoming premier of Egypt, responsible for leading the nation through a famine.

1. Mary (Luke 1 and 2): We don't know a lot about Mary's life, but we do know that she was poor. When she and Joseph presented Jesus at the Temple in Jerusalem, they offered the sacrifice of those who could not afford a lamb. She lived in Nazareth — not a thriving metropolis. When the angel came to Mary to announce that God had chosen her to be the mother of his Son, even Mary was surprised. Why would God choose a poor virgin from a nothing town? But God does not look at the surface. Instead, he looks into the heart.

VILLAINS

The Bible is the story of the relationship between human be-
ings and God. Since it depicts the reality of human life, it in-
cludes both good and bad. In addition to its heroes, the Bible
includes some of the worst villains history has ever known.

10. Nebuchadnezzar (Daniel 1–4): Nebuchadnezzar was
the king of Babylon who defeated Judah and took its citizens into exile. He tried to assimilate some of the exiles into
the kingdom of Babylon, but for him, assimilation meant
abandoning the one true God to worship multiple gods.
Those who refused to bow down to an idol were put to
death by being tossed into a furnace. Nebuchadnezzar was
redeemed, however, by his willingness to recognize God's
power after God had saved the three Israelites from the fire.

9. Haman (Esther): Haman was a chief adviser to King
Ahasuerus, the husband of Queen Esther. Haman was very
proud of his position and took offense at anything he per-
ceived as an insult. Because Mordecai (Esther's foster father)
and the other Jews would not kneel to him, Haman hatched
a plan to kill the Jewish people living in Persia. Esther put
her own life on the line to thwart his plan, ultimately turning it against him so that the Jewish people were saved and
Haman was executed.

8. Abimelech (Judges 8:29–9:57): Abimelech was one of the seventy (!) sons of the great judge Gideon. He's proof positive that sometimes the fruit falls far from the tree. He began his rule by killing all but one of his brothers to make sure they didn't challenge him. Under his rule, Israel wandered far from the covenant. Eventually, the prominent men who supported his murder of his brothers turned on him and attempted to kill him. Abimelech was severely wounded when a woman dropped a millstone on his head. Rather than be killed by a woman, Abimelech had one of his followers kill him.

7. Pilate (Matthew 27:11–26; Mark 15:1–15; Luke 23:1–25; John 18:28–19:16): Pilate governed the territory of Judea on behalf of the Roman Empire. Scholars may debate his historical role, but in the Bible he does one thing: he condemns Jesus to death by crucifixion. The scriptural accounts are very clear. Pilate did not believe that Jesus was guilty of a capital crime. Pilate condemned Jesus because it was the easy choice — a choice that allowed him to avoid conflict with the local leaders. His villainy lay in choosing what is easy over what is right.

6. Ahab and Jezebel (1 Kings 21): Ahab was the King of Israel during the time when Elijah was prophesying. Influenced by his wife, Jezebel, Ahab abandoned worship of the one true God and began to worship Baal. But Ahab and Jezebel did not only abandon God. When Ahab was unsuccessful in purchasing a vineyard owned by a man named Naboth, Jezebel arranged for Naboth's murder. Ahab and Jezebel focused solely on their own desires with no regard for God or human beings. The name "Jezebel" has become synonymous with an evil woman.

5. Pharaoh (Exodus 1–14): Pharaoh, the ruler of Egypt, was the agent of Israel's oppression. Though the Israelites were originally welcome guests in Egypt, over time the Egyptians grew concerned about the Israelites' growing numbers. Pharaoh took increasingly harsh measures against the Hebrew people, condemning them to lives of servitude and instituting a policy of killing their male children. When Moses came and asked that the Israelites be freed, Pharaoh hardened his heart to this request, despite the many displays of God's power in the plagues. Even after the killing of the firstborn convinced Pharaoh to let the Israelites go, he changed his mind and chased them into the desert. His pursuit was halted only when the Egyptian army drowned in the Red Sea.

4. Antiochus Epiphanes (1 and 2 Maccabees): Antiochus Epiphanes ruled Israel during the Hellenic (Greek) Empire. He ruthlessly suppressed the practice of Judaism, killing and torturing anyone who continued to live according to God's law. People were executed for owning copies of the Torah, for circumcising their sons, and for refusing to eat unclean food. Antiochus Epiphanes even desecrated the Temple, placing a statue of a pagan god in the Holy of Holies (the holiest part of the Temple). As punishment for his villainy, Antiochus Epiphanes died alone in a country far from home.

3. Herod (see especially Matthew 2 and 14:3–12; Mark 6:17–29): Two rulers named Herod are mentioned in the Gospels. Herod the Great and Herod Antipas were father and son — and evil seems to have been a family trait. Herod the Great was visited by the magi after Jesus' birth. Fearing the threat of the newborn King of the Jews, Herod ordered the murder of every male child younger than two, an unthinkable massacre. His son Herod Antipas was responsible for the murder of John the Baptist. Herod Antipas had imprisoned John because John spoke out against Herod's marriage to his brother's wife, Herodias. When Herodias' daughter performed a dance at a banquet, Herod promised her the gift of her choice. She asked for the head of John the Baptist. Rather than look weak before his courtiers, Herod acceded to her request and executed John.

2. Judas (Matthew 26:14–16, 20–25, 47–56, 27:3–10; Mark 14:10–11, 17–21, 43–52; Luke 22:1–6, 21–23, 47–53; John 13–21–30, 18:1–11): Judas was one of the Twelve Apostles chosen personally by Jesus and closest to him. In spite of this close relationship, Judas went to the chief priests and offered to hand Jesus over to them. In exchange for thirty pieces of silver, Judas led the guards to Jesus so that they could arrest him. Matthew's Gospel tells us that Judas regretted his actions, but rather than turn to the mercy of God, Judas despaired and ended his own life.

1. Satan (see especially Job, Revelation, Matthew 4:1–11, Mark 1:12–13, Luke 4:1–13): There is no question about the greatest villain in Scripture. He is called by many names: Beelzebub, Satan, or simply the Evil One. He tempts people to abandon their faith, to ignore those in need, and to disobey God. His path leads to everlasting death.

BLESSED ARE THE PEACEMAKERS

While there are certainly plenty of battles in the Bible (see the top ten list in Part Three for some examples), many of the people we meet in Scripture try to bring peace, bridging differences and seeking reconciliation.

10. The Good Scribe (Mark 12:28–34): In Mark's telling of the Two Great Commandments, the scribe who questions Jesus was not trying to trip Jesus up or create a controversy. Instead, he was trying to grow in understanding and knowledge, the foundations of peace. When Jesus responded to his questions, he affirmed and embraced Jesus' teaching. Jesus told him that he was near to the Kingdom of God. Those who seek peace must question with an open mind and be willing to learn.

9. Abraham (Genesis 13): When Abraham left his family's homeland to travel to the land of Canaan, his kinsman Lot traveled with him. Soon after their migration, difficulties began to emerge because the land could not support both men and their households. Rather than fight about the distribution of the land, Abraham acted with generosity, offering Lot his choice of land, agreeing to take the portion Lot rejected. Such generosity and self-denial are important characteristics of those who seek peace.

8. Moses (see especially Exodus 32): Moses frequently acted as a peacemaker between God and the Israelite people. During their wanderings in the desert, the Israelites frequently became impatient, challenging and second-guessing God. When God became angry with the people, Moses speaks on the people's behalf, seeking mercy and another chance. Like all peacemakers, Moses knows that, without forgiveness, peace is impossible.

7. Gamaliel (Acts 5:17–42): In the days after the Pentecost, the Apostles preached boldly in the Temple precincts, stirring up anger among the Jewish authorities. Ultimately, they were arrested and brought before the Sanhedrin. Gamaliel, a respected leader of the Jewish community, interceded on their behalf. He pointed out that if the Apostles were acting on behalf of God they would certainly be successful. If they were not acting in response to a call from God, they would fail. To find true peace, we must act in accord with God's plans. Otherwise we may find ourselves fighting God, a fight we cannot win.

6. Joseph (Genesis 42–45): Joseph certainly had good reason to be angry with his brothers. After all, they had sold him into slavery! Yet when he found himself in a situation where he held the power of life and death over them, he did not exploit his position. He made sure that they had what they needed, and he offered them an opportunity for reconciliation. Peacemakers cannot hold a grudge or misuse their power.

5. Peter and James (Acts 15): In the years after Jesus' Resurrection, the early Church had some growing pains. One of the first major conflicts was whether Gentile converts to Christianity were obliged to follow all of the Jewish law, including the requirement that all males be circumcised. The leaders of the Church gathered in Jerusalem to discuss the question. During this meeting, called the Council of Jerusalem, Peter and James took the leading role, seeking a path that would bring people to Christ, the source of peace.

4. Mary (the Gospels): For a person of such impact, Mary gets relatively few verses in the Gospels. That makes it even more interesting that two of her actions that are recounted deal with her care for others. First, in the early days of her own pregnancy, she traveled to visit Elizabeth who is in the late stages of pregnancy at an advanced age. Second, at the beginning of Jesus' public ministry, her concern for the bride and groom prompted Jesus' first miracle at the wedding in Cana. True peace is always based in authentic concern for others.

3. Lady Wisdom (Proverbs, Wisdom, Sirach): The Bible presents Wisdom, personified as a woman, as the ideal companion for anyone who wishes to be successful and holy. Making a friend of Wisdom means that one's life will be well-ordered and at peace. Most important, by seeking Wisdom, we will grow closer to God. True peace is found by pursuing Wisdom rather than the trappings of worldly success.

2. Holy Spirit (see especially John 14–17): God sends the Spirit into the world to bring peace. Saint Paul even taught that peace is a fruit of the Holy Spirit (cf. Galatians 5:22–23). God is the true source of all peace. If we live in the Spirit, seeking the things of the Spirit rather than of the world, we will do good for others, love God beyond all things, and help to bring peace to the world.

1. Jesus: Jesus's lasting gift to his followers is his peace. Jesus was careful to qualify that the peace he gives is not the peace of the world — often merely an absence of strife. The peace Jesus brings is much more profound. The peace of Christ is founded on his self-sacrifice, his death on the cross. Through his saving death, Jesus makes it possible for us to live in the peace of God forever.

PROPHETS, NOT PROFITS

Contrary to popular opinion, a prophet does not necessarily foretell the future. Instead, a prophet speaks on behalf of God, delivering the messages entrusted by God. They give messages of warning, comfort, instruction, and challenge. [Note: The Scripture citations are noted only when the prophet does not have a book named for him.]

10. Joel: Joel calls upon the people to read the signs of the times and reform their lives. Nothing should take priority over a return to the Lord. When the people return to the Lord, God will pour out his Spirit in abundance and call all people to himself.

9. Nathan (2 Samuel 7–12): The prophet Nathan advises King David. He gives David two important messages from the Lord. First, Nathan conveys God's promise that a son of David will rule over a kingdom that has no end. The second message calls David to repentance after his adultery with Bathsheba and his murder of her husband. Nathan is, in many ways, the "conscience of the king."

8. Amos: Amos prophesied to the people of the Northern Kingdom (the land called Israel made up of the land held by ten of the tribes, as opposed to the Southern Kingdom, or Judah, the land held by two of the tribes). God called Amos from his work as a sheep herder to call Israel to reform. His messages speak of the importance of fidelity to the Lord's covenant and living in justice and charity. He is particularly sharp with the rich who take advantage of the poor and wallow in excess.

7. Hosea: Hosea's marriage to Gomer provides a metaphor for his prophetic preaching. Their initial love is damaged by infidelity, but ultimately, the couple is reunited. In the same way, the early days of the covenant gave way to Israel's infidelity in worshipping other gods. In the end, however, Israel will repent and return to the Lord. Then, God will restore them.

6. Samuel (1 Samuel 1–25): Samuel was the last of the judges as well as a great prophet. While he was still a child, his parents dedicated him to service of the Lord at the sanctuary in Shiloh. God began speaking to him while he was still very young. He anointed the first two kings of Israel, Saul and David. He served as an advisor to Saul, constantly encouraging him to be faithful to the covenant.

5. Ezekiel: Ezekiel was a priest before he was a prophet. Along with other leading members of the community, he went into exile in Babylon when Jerusalem fell. He is a prophet of God's omnipotence. God is always in control. Even when he punishes the people harshly, it is always for the sake of his name and to call people into renewed fidelity. They will have a new heart and a new spirit.

4. Jeremiah: Jeremiah received his call as a prophet when he was still a young man. His prophetic ministry took place in a difficult period in the history of Judah, the time surrounding the capture of Jerusalem by the Babylonians and the exile. As was true of many prophets, Jeremiah reminded the people that if they were not faithful to the covenant, worshipping the Lord alone, the nation would suffer. Jeremiah's prophecy was met with insult and scorn. He was arrested and even threatened with death. Jeremiah wanted to stop prophesying, but the word of God burned in him until he spoke it. When Israel fell, Jeremiah offered the exiles and those left behind words of comfort.

3. Elijah (1 Kings 17–2 Kings 2): Elijah was the prophet by whom all other prophets were measured! He preached in the Northern Kingdom — rebuking unjust kings and proclaiming that the Lord is the only true God. He encountered God on Mount Horeb and battled the prophets of Baal on Mount Carmel. Elijah did not die. He was taken alive into heaven in a fiery chariot.

2. Isaiah: Isaiah's call as a prophet came in the midst of a vision of God's power and glory. Compared to God, human beings are weak and sinful. Yet Isaiah proclaimed messages of hope, where God would rule in a world where all lived in peace, giving comfort to the faithful and forgiving them their sins. The poetic messages of this prophet are among the most beautiful and memorable in all of Scripture.

1. John the Baptist (Matthew 3; Mark 1; Luke 1 and 3; John 1): John was the last of the prophets. As most prophets did, he called the people to repentance, calling them to live justly and to love the Lord. He baptized those who accepted his challenge in the Jordan River. Most importantly, John pointed to the one who would come after him — the Messiah, Jesus.

TEACHERS

Disciples are learners, and learners need teachers. The Bible gives us great examples of people who teach others how to live lives of justice and fidelity to the Lord.

10. Eli (1 Samuel 2–3): Eli was a priest of the sanctuary in Shiloh. When Hannah and Elkanah dedicated their son Samuel to service in the sanctuary, Eli became his teacher. Eli taught Samuel his duties in the sanctuary. More importantly, he taught him how to listen and respond to the voice of the Lord.

9. Solomon (1 Kings 10): Solomon was known for his wisdom. He was so renowned that other rulers traveled from great distances to learn from him. His most famous visitor was the Queen of Sheba. She came to Jerusalem with a huge entourage, overwhelmingly rich presents — and a list of tough questions. Solomon answered all of her questions, convincing the queen that his reputation as a wise teacher and ruler was well-earned.

8. Peter (Acts of the Apostles, especially chapters 2 and 3): Immediately after Pentecost, Peter emerged as the leader of the Apostles, stepping forward to preach and teach about Jesus. Drawing on the Scriptures of the Jewish people (what we call the Old Testament), he proclaimed Jesus as the fulfillment of prophecy and the Messiah sent by God. He was such an effective teacher that three thousand people sought baptism after his preaching.

7. Mary and Joseph (Matthew 1–2; Luke 1–2): We know very little about Jesus' childhood. In fact, the years before Jesus' public ministry begins are often called "the hidden years." But we can assume that Mary and Joseph were Jesus' most important childhood teachers. Luke tells us that Jesus "grew and became strong, filled with wisdom" (Luke 2:40). Likely Jesus learned a trade. He certainly learned to read the Scriptures in Hebrew and to obey the Law so that he could live a righteous life. Joseph and Mary were his models of living.

6. Ben Sira (Wisdom of Ben Sira): Ben Sira was a great teacher who lived in the second century before Christ. A great lover of Wisdom, Ben Sira wrote a book "so that those who love learning might, by accepting what he had written, make even greater progress in living, according to the Law" (Foreword, Wisdom of Ben Sira). His writings discuss all facets of life and serve as a practical manual for living.

5. Lois and Eunice (2 Timothy 1:5): Though mentioned only in this single verse, we know a surprising amount about these women. The grandmother and mother of Timothy, these women nurtured his faith in Christ. Like all good teachers, they helped him find and follow the vocation to which God called him.

4. Wisdom (see especially Proverbs and Wisdom 6): The Bible teaches that gaining Wisdom is always the goal of learning. In several books of the Old Testament, Wisdom is personified as a woman who passes "into holy souls from age to age, / she produces friends of God and prophets" (Wisdom 7:27). Befriending Wisdom, seeking her always, provides the best teacher and leads the learner to God.

3. Philip (Acts 8): At the Lord's direction, Philip was traveling from Jerusalem to Gaza when he came upon an Ethiopian official traveling along the same route. Once again directed by the Lord, Philip approached the official to ask what he was reading. The official had been reading one of the Songs of the Suffering Servant from the Book of the Prophet Isaiah, and he questioned Philip about the meaning of the text. Philip explained the text in reference to Jesus, discussing Jesus' saving death and Resurrection. So compelling was his teaching that the official sought baptism immediately. This story shows that a committed teacher and an inquisitive student are an unbeatable combination.

2. Paul (Acts of the Apostles and Pauline Letters): Paul was a master teacher, using preaching and writing, always starting with his audience's understanding. He taught Jewish crowds by explaining that Jesus was the Messiah promised by Scripture. When facing Gentile crowds, his arguments were based on philosophy and common examples, using metaphors like family relationships and the human body. He was an indefatigable teacher — traveling almost constantly and facing innumerable hardships to fulfill his mission.

1. Jesus (Gospels): Teacher was the title given to Jesus by his disciples, and even by some of his opponents. Jesus taught throughout Galilee and Judea, using sermons, parables, and miraculous deeds. Whether preaching to a huge crowd or explaining things to his Apostles privately, Jesus always drew his listeners to the truth, knowing that by embracing the truth they would draw closer to him. And when he ascended back to his Father in heaven, he sent his Spirit to continue his teaching.

BIBLICAL PEOPLE YOU SHOULD KNOW (BUT PROBABLY DON'T)

The Bible is filled with wonderful characters that are interest-ing and important, even if their stories are told in only a few verses. Let's look at some of these more obscure personalities and what they have to say to us.

10. Simon the Magician (Acts 8:9–25): As you might guess from his name, Simon practiced magic for a living, en-chanting people in Samaria with the tricks he performed. Moved by the preaching of Philip, he decided to embrace Christianity. After his conversion, Peter and John came to Samaria to lay hands on the people so that they would re-ceive the Holy Spirit. Simon was so impressed by this action that he offered to pay Peter and John if they would teach him the "trick." Peter refused his request harshly, making it clear that the power of God is not for sale. Faced with this rebuke, Simon asked forgiveness. However, he lent his name to the crime of simony — the selling of sacraments.

9. Onesimus (Philemon): Onesimus is the runaway slave of Philemon. He met Paul while Paul was imprisoned and converted to Christianity. After the conversion, Paul wrote a letter to Philemon, asking him to accept Onesimus back, not only as a slave, but as a brother in the Lord. Paul also seemed to want Philemon to release Onesimus for service of the Gospel. In making his argument, Paul pointed out that, since he brought Philemon to Christ, Philemon owes him his life. And that, my friends, is the first recorded use of Catholic guilt.

8. Huldah (2 Kings 22:14–20; 2 Chronicles 34:22–28): Huldah was a prophetess in Judah during the reign of Josiah. Josiah had just found the Book of the Law and was dismayed by the lack of faith in Judah, so he sent a delegation to Huldah to consult the Lord through her. Huldah reported that calamity would come upon Israel, but that it would not happen during Josiah's lifetime because he had humbled himself before the Lord. Huldah was part of the long line of prophets reminding the people of Israel that their political fortunes were tied to their fidelity to the covenant.

7. Lydia (Acts 16:11–15): Lydia lived in Philippi on the Greek peninsula. As a seller of purple cloth, she catered to the wealthy of the community and was likely rather well-to-do herself. She was in attendance when Paul preached to the women of Philippi and was moved deeply by what he had to say. She and her household became Christian and sought baptism. She extended an invitation for Paul and his company to stay in her home during their visit to Philippi, offering them the gift of hospitality.

6. Baruch (Baruch): Baruch served as a secretary and assistant to the prophet Jeremiah, writing and carrying his letters and performing other helpful tasks. When Jeremiah was barred from the Temple, Baruch entered and read messages dictated by Jeremiah, delivering the words of the Lord. The Book of the Prophet Baruch is attributed to him and is set during the Babylonian exile.

5. Susanna and Joanna (Luke 8:1–4): These two women are identified as members of the group of women who followed Jesus in his ministry through Galilee and Judea, supporting this ministry from their resources. Their support was essential to Jesus and his Apostles being able to continue their work of preaching and healing.

4. Naaman (2 Kings 5:1–27): Naaman was a commander in the army of the King of Aram. Though successful and highly respected, Naaman was a leper. An Israelite girl serving in his household suggested that he visit the prophet Elisha to seek a cure for his leprosy. Naaman traveled to Israel bearing rich gifts and a letter from the King of Aram to the King of Israel, requesting a cure. Though the King of Israel was dismayed by the request, Elisha sent Naaman a message telling him to wash seven times in the Jordan to cure his leprosy. At first, Naaman rejected this suggestion, wanting a more impressive miraculous cure. Finally, after much convincing, Naaman followed Elisha's directions and was cured. Naaman returned to Elisha's home and offered him gifts in gratitude for the cure, but Elisha refused his offer. Instead, Naaman took two loads of earth to build an altar so that he could worship the Lord.

3. Cornelius (Acts 10): Cornelius was a Roman soldier, noted for his respect for the tenets of Judaism, his devout prayer life, and his generosity in giving alms. God spoke to him in a vision, telling him to invite Peter to his home. When Peter arrived, Cornelius welcomed him warmly. Peter explained that, while a devout Jew should not visit the home of a Gentile, God had sent him a vision clarifying that no one should be considered unclean. Peter preached the Gospel of Jesus Christ to Cornelius and his household. The

Holy Spirit descended on the household and they were baptized into Christ.

2. Priscilla and Aquila (Acts 18; Romans 16): Priscilla and Aquila were a Jewish husband and wife exiled from Rome when the Jews were expelled from that city. Since, like Paul, they were tentmakers by trade, Paul stayed with them when he was in Corinth. The Church in Corinth met in their home, and Paul recounts that they risked their lives on his behalf.

1. Nicodemus (John 3 and 19): Nicodemus was a Pharisee and held a high position among the Jews, possibly even serving on the Sanhedrin. He first came to Jesus at night and expressed his belief that Jesus was a teacher sent by God. Jesus began to teach him, answering Nicodemus' questions and explaining the gift of new life in the Spirit. After this nighttime teaching session, we do not see Nicodemus again until the day of Jesus' death. After Jesus dies, John tells us that Nicodemus came to help bury Jesus, bringing a quantity of aloe and spices (a rich gift) to anoint the body. Clearly, his faith in and love for Jesus had remained intact.

TWO

PLACES AND EVENTS

THERE'S MORE THAN ONE RESURRECTION IN THE BIBLE?

Most human beings fear death, the end of life as we know it. However, in the Old and New Testaments, people are raised from the dead, demonstrating that God is more powerful than death.

10. The Shunamite Couple's Son (2 Kings 4:8–37): A husband and wife in the town of Shunam extended gracious hospitality to the prophet Elisha. Because of their great kindness, the Lord gave them the child they had long desired. Unfortunately, while he was still very young, the couple's son fell ill and died. Seeing the mother's anguish over the loss of her precious child, Elisha raised the boy from the dead and gave him back to his parents.

9. Elijah and the Widow's Son (1 Kings 17:7–24): During a time of drought and famine, Elijah approached a widow and asked her for something to eat. The widow demurred, stating that she had almost no food left for her and her son. Once that food was gone, they would die of starvation. Elijah assured her that, if she shared what she had with him, the Lord would not let her and her son go hungry. She gave Elijah some food and all three — the widow, her son, and Elijah — had enough to eat until the famine ended. However, during the time of the drought, the son became ill and died. Because of Elijah's prayers, the Lord raised the boy from the dead. This great miracle convinced the widow that Elijah was truly a prophet of God.

8. Eutychus (Acts 20:7–12): One night, Paul was preaching in Troas. Paul spoke for a very long time — past midnight — and a young boy named Eutychus fell asleep during his preaching. Unfortunately for Eutychus, he was sitting in the window sill and, when he fell asleep, he fell out of the window — three stories up. Paul rushed to the boy and was able to raise him from the dead. Surely, Eutychus never slept through another homily.

7. Tabitha/Dorcas (Acts 9:36–43): While Peter was traveling in Joppa, he was brought to the home of a woman named Tabitha who had died recently. Tabitha seems to have been a leading member of the Christian community, and she was noted for her generosity and kindness. Through the power of God, Peter was able to restore her to life. This miracle encouraged many people in the region to convert to Christianity.

6. Jairus's daughter (Matthew 9:1–26; Mark 5:21–43; Luke 8:11–56): Jairus, a leader in his local synagogue, approached Jesus because his only child, a daughter, was extremely ill. He asked Jesus to come and heal her. Unfortunately, before Jesus could get there, the girl died. Jesus encouraged Jairus to have faith and continued to his house. Once Jesus arrived, he announced that the girl was sleeping, not dead, occasioning the mockery of those who had gathered to mourn. Taking only the girl's parents, Peter, James, and John into the room where the body rested, Jesus raised her to life. He told her parents to give her something to eat in order to demonstrate to those gathered that the girl was truly alive.

5. Son of Widow of Nain (Luke 7:11–17): In the course of their travels, Jesus and his disciples came upon the funeral procession for the only son of a widow. With neither son nor husband for support, this woman would likely be condemned to a life of abject poverty. Moved with pity for her plight, Jesus stopped the procession and raised the son from the dead. This miraculous act amazed and frightened the townspeople and those who were following Jesus, and they became convinced that Jesus was a prophet.

4. Lazarus (John 11): Jesus had a close, friendly relationship with Mary, Martha, and Lazarus, siblings who lived in the town of Bethany near Jerusalem. Jesus and his disciples seem to have stayed in the siblings' home on at least a few occasions. So, when Lazarus became seriously ill, his sisters called Jesus to come to him. Jesus stayed where he was for two days after receiving this summons. The disciples did not want him to go to Bethany even then, because they were afraid that the Jewish leaders would try to have Jesus killed. By the time Jesus got to Bethany, Lazarus had been dead and buried for four days. Upon seeing Jesus' grief over Lazarus's death, the people who had come to mourn with Mary and Martha began to question why Jesus had done nothing to help his dear friend, Lazarus. In response, Jesus prayed to his Father and raised Lazarus from the dead, calling him from the tomb.

3. Saints (Matthew 27:51–54): Matthew's Gospel recounts many miraculous events that occurred at the moment Jesus died on the cross, including an earthquake and the tearing of the veil in the Holy of Holies in the Temple. Matthew says that after Jesus' death many holy people who had died rose from the dead and were seen walking around Jerusalem. By his death, Jesus broke the bonds of death, once and for all.

2. The Just (see especially Wisdom, Daniel, 1 Corinthians, Revelation): Scripture teaches that those who are just, though they die, will be raised to eternal life with God on the last day. The saving death of Jesus defeated death and will allow those who are faithful to Christ to live with God forever in heaven.

1. Jesus (Matthew 28; Mark 16; Luke 24; John 20): The most important resurrection in all of Scripture is the Resurrection of Jesus Christ. This Resurrection destroyed death forever, once again opening the gates of heaven to all who believe. On the morning of the first day of the week (Sunday, the day after the Sabbath), several women went to Jesus' tomb to anoint his body for burial. The fast approaching Sabbath had not left sufficient time for Jesus' body to be anointed before burial. However, when the women arrived at the tomb, they did not find Jesus' body. Instead, angels announced to them that Jesus had been raised from the dead. Filled with amazement, joy, and fear, the women ran off to share this Good News with the Apostles.

JOURNEYING FAR AND WIDE

The events of the Bible take place in a rather small expanse of land. Despite the geographic limits, people spend a lot of time traveling from one place to another. Many of these journeys are fraught with meaning and hold lessons for us.

10. The Magi's Journey (Matthew 2): All we know about the magi's journey is that it started "in the east" and ended in Bethlehem (with a stop in Jerusalem), following the course of a star. We should ponder the faith, courage, and commitment it took the magi to leave the comfort of their homes for the dangers and difficulties of travel. But their reward was great: they met Christ.

9. Joseph to Egypt (Genesis 37 and 50): Joseph's journey to Egypt wasn't voluntary. He had been sold into slavery by his brothers. Though his time in Egypt did not begin well (he spent time in prison), Joseph made the best of his gifts and circumstances and rose to become Pharaoh's second in command. This position enabled him to save his father and his brothers and their families during a time of famine. He grew to understand that God made the bad in his trip to Egypt turn out for the good.

8. The Flight to Egypt (Matthew 2): Warned by an angel that Herod was trying to kill Jesus, Joseph took Mary and Jesus to Egypt, out of the reach of Herod's wrath. Even with an angel's assurances, a trip across a desert with a small child and a nursing mother must have been a challenging journey, followed by all the difficulties of establishing a new life in a foreign land.

7. Mary's Travels While Pregnant (Luke 1–2): The Gospel of Luke recounts two trips by Mary while she was pregnant with Jesus. First, soon after Jesus was conceived, she traveled from Nazareth to Judea to visit her kinswoman Elizabeth, pregnant with John (who would become the Baptist), staying for several months before returning home. As the time for the birth drew near, she once again traveled from Nazareth to Judea, this time to Bethlehem. These trips are not onerous by modern terms, but in the first century, while pregnant, they had to have been quite challenging. That Mary made them speaks to her care for Elizabeth and her inner strength.

6. Return from Exile (Ezra and Nehemiah; Psalm 126): For the Israelites returning from exile in Babylon, seeing Jerusalem again was like a dream come true. Under their political and religious leaders, the people immediately set about rebuilding the city and the Temple and restoring order. A key part of the restoration was a renewed fidelity to the covenant. Through their trials, the Israelites had come to understand that when they lived in right relationship with God the rest of their lives were ordered rightly as well.

5. Abraham to Canaan (Genesis 12): Abraham's story began when God called him to leave his father's home and go to a new land. God promised Abraham that his trust would be rewarded. He would become a great nation, and other nations would find blessing in him. As always, Abraham placed his trust in God, and he went to Canaan. Similarly, our faith in God must underlie all our decisions.

4. Emmaus (Luke 24): On the afternoon of Jesus' Resurrection, two of his disciples traveled from Jerusalem to Emmaus. (Interestingly, only one of the two is named — Cleopas.) Jesus joined them on their journey, though they did not recognize him. As they walked, they discussed the Crucifixion and the reports of the Resurrection. Jesus used the journey to teach them, helping them to understand what the Scriptures said about the Messiah. As they came to the end of their journey, they invited Jesus to stay with them for the night, and he revealed his true nature to them in the breaking of the bread.

3. Paul's Missionary Journeys (Acts 13–28): Following his conversion, Paul took three extended journeys to preach the Gospel. These journeys took him all over Asia Minor and included multiple imprisonments and three shipwrecks. [Travel note: If you board a ship and Saint Paul is on board, you may want to sail later.] Yet Paul teaches us that preaching the Gospel is worth any hardship.

2. The Exodus (Exodus to Joshua 4): Liberated from slavery in Egypt, the Israelites undertook the exodus — the great journey from Egypt to the Promised Land. Because of the Israelites' lack of faith, God decided that the journey would take forty years so that the faithless ones would not enter the Promised Land. The journey was long and arduous, punctuated by battles and failures. Yet through it all, God showed his faithfulness and power, parting the Red Sea, offering the covenant, and protecting the people he had made his own.

1. Via Dolorosa (Matthew 27; Mark 15; Luke 23; John 19): The Way of Sorrows. The path Jesus walked on his way to crucifixion on Calvary. The path we recall when celebrating the Stations of the Cross. No other journey is fraught with such pain or with such hope, for by his saving death, Jesus opened for us the gates of heaven so that we may live forever.

MIRACLES

Miracles are events that cannot be explained by natural causes. Miracles change the pattern of the natural world to show the power and majesty of God.

10. Cure of the Ten Lepers (Luke 17:11–19): Only Luke recounts this story of ten lepers who seek healing from Jesus. Jesus sent them to the priests who had to verify the cure so that the lepers would be readmitted to the community. While the lepers were on their way, they were cured. Of the ten, only one returned to thank Jesus — a Samaritan, an outsider, a religious outcast. Ninety percent of the lepers failed to thank God for the gift of healing. What percentage of the time do we fail to express gratitude for God's gifts?

9. Healing of the Man Born Blind (John 9): In his travels, Jesus came across a man born blind and healed him to show the power of God. Jesus made mud, smeared the mud on the man's eyes, and told him to wash away the mud. When the mud was gone, the man could see. This healing caused a dispute with the religious leaders because it took place on the Sabbath (making mud violated the laws of the Sabbath). Under questioning from the religious authorities, the man remained firm in his account of Jesus' actions and, upon learning that Jesus was the Messiah, he offered him worship.

8. Walking on the Water (Matthew 14:22–33; Mark 6:45–52; John 6:16–21): Jesus had stayed ashore to pray while his disciples sailed across the lake. During the night, Jesus appeared to the disciples, walking on the water. The disciples were shocked and feared that the vision was a ghost. To confirm Jesus' identity, Peter asked that he be allowed to walk on the water as well. Jesus agreed, but when Peter began walking on the lake, his fears overcame him and he began to sink, only to be rescued by Jesus. Fear and the lack of faith limit our experience of God's miraculous power.

7. Healing of a Woman with a Hemorrhage (Matthew 9:20–22; Mark 5:25–34; Luke 8:43–48): This unnamed woman suffered from a hemorrhage for twelve years. Because of the laws of ritual purity, this ailment would have separated her from the ordinary activities of the community. In her desperation, she joined the crowds around Jesus and simply touched the hem of his clothing. Jesus' power was so great that such a glancing touch cured her. Jesus felt the power go out from him and questioned the crowd. The woman courageously stepped forward and told Jesus her story. Jesus commended her for her faith and sent her on her way. A little faith goes a long way.

6. Cure of the Beggar at the Beautiful Gate (Acts 3): In the days after Pentecost, Peter and John went to the Temple for afternoon prayer. At the Beautiful Gate, they encountered a beggar who was unable to walk. Peter cured the man in the name of Jesus. The man entered the Temple, leaping and singing God's praise while Peter and John were called before the religious authorities to answer for their actions. This miracle recalls that those who bear the name Christian are called to show God's power before the nations.

5. Changing Water into Wine (John 2:1–11): Jesus, his mother, and his disciples attended a wedding in Cana. When the wine ran short, Mary asked Jesus to help the couple avoid embarrassment. Jesus had the servants fill large vessels with water which he then turned into high-quality wine that the wedding guests enjoy. This first miracle evidenced Jesus' power to his disciples and enlivened their faith in him.

4. Calming of a Storm (Matthew 8:23–27; Mark 4:35–40; Luke 8:22–25): As the disciples were sailing across the sea, a violent storm arose, threatening to sink the boat. In spite of the storm's violence and the imminent danger, Jesus remained asleep in the boat. Awakened by the panicking disciples, Jesus calmed the sea with a word, amazing the disciples with his power over nature.

3. Manna in the Desert (Exodus 16): As the Israelites traveled through the desert on their way from Egypt to the Promised Land, they complained to Moses about the lack of food. In response, God sent manna to feed the people. Manna, a substance previously unknown, appeared each morning, lying on the ground like frost. Manna could be baked or boiled and tasted like cakes made with honey. God provides for our every need.

2. Parting of the Red Sea (Exodus 14): In their escape from slavery in Egypt, the Israelites seemed to be caught in an impossible situation. On one side was the Red Sea and on the other was Pharaoh's army. The Israelites couldn't move forward, and they couldn't go back. God commanded Moses to hold his staff over the water, and God sent a wind across the surface of the water, clearing a path through the center. The Israelites walked into the midst of the sea, following a path of dry land with the water walled up on either side. When the Egyptians tried to follow the Israelites through the sea, God let the water flow back over them, destroying the entire army and convincing the Israelites that the Lord is a mighty God.

1. Feeding the Five Thousand (Matthew 14:5–21; Mark 6:32–44; Luke 9:10–17; John 6:1–13): Huge crowds followed Jesus to listen to him preach. On one occasion, the disciples expressed concern that the crowd would not be able to find food in the area. Jesus told the disciples that they should feed the crowds. When the disciples protested that only five loaves and two fish were available, Jesus told the disciples to instruct the people to sit down. Jesus blessed the small amount of food available and asked the disciples to distribute it to the people. Not only were five loaves and two fish enough to feed the crowd, but there were twelve baskets of food left over. God's miraculous love is more abundant than our needs.

SQUARE MEALS

There's a lot of eating in the Bible! Jesus does much of his teaching while gathered with his disciples and others at table. Other meals have symbolic meaning. Scripture uses this common human activity to convey important messages.

10. Belshazzar's Banquet (Daniel 5): Belshazzar was a king of Babylon during the time of the Jewish exile in Babylon. One night, he invited leading citizens of the city to a banquet in the palace. As a special feature of the event, he used the sacred vessels captured from the Temple in Jerusalem to serve his guests. During this profane banquet, a disembodied hand appeared, writing on the wall. Daniel was brought in to interpret the writing. Daniel explained that, because Belshazzar had shown such disrespect to God in using the sacred vessels this way, his rule had been found wanting and would be cut short. Belshazzar was killed that night. This event is the origin of the saying "to see the handwriting on the wall."

9. Passover at Gilgal (Joshua 5:10–12): After the Hebrew people crossed into the Promised Land near Gilgal, they settled into camp and celebrated Passover. Immediately after Passover, they began to eat the produce of the land of Canaan. Once the Israelites could survive off the produce of the land, God's gifts of manna and quail ceased. In our need, God always provides.

8. Peter's Vision (Acts 10:9–16): While staying in the home of Simon the tanner, Peter had a vision of unclean animals and heard a voice telling him to slaughter and eat the animals. Peter objected because he followed the law regarding clean and unclean foods with great care. The Lord told Peter that he declared these foods clean. While this vision was not an actual meal, it communicated clearly to Peter that the Gentiles who wanted to follow Christ were not required to follow the Law of Moses in its entirety. Gentiles were to be welcomed into the Church with open arms. This development was critical to the growth of the Church.

7. Abraham Feeding His Guests (Genesis 18): Three visitors arrive while Abraham and his household camp in Mamre. Abraham welcomes these unexpected guests immediately, inviting them to rest in the shade and instructing his servants to prepare a meal. This meal is no light snack! He serves them meat, bread, milk, and curds — a veritable banquet! Only later does Abraham learn that his guests are angels, sent to announce the birth of his son, Isaac. Abraham serves as a model of generous hospitality.

6. Post-Resurrection Meals (Luke 24; John 21): Both Luke and John recount appearances by Jesus after his Resurrection. In Luke's Gospel, Jesus asks his disciples for something to eat, and they give him some baked fish. In John's Gospel, Jesus appears in the early morning, after a group of disciples have spent the night fishing. Jesus calls the disciples to the breakfast he has prepared. Since only living beings eat, Jesus actions evidence to his disciples that he truly is alive!

5. Meal on the Mountain (Isaiah 25:6–9): The prophet Isaiah speaks of the day when God will deliver Israel from all its foes. On this day, Jerusalem will celebrate. As Isaiah describes this celebration, God will provide a sumptuous banquet of the finest food and wine. All people will be invited to share in this banquet. But God's bountiful love will extend even farther. God will put an end to sadness and death, redeeming his people. The image presented by Isaiah is a precursor of the heavenly banquet to which we are called.

4. Dinner at the Home of Levi (Matthew 9:9–13; Luke 5:27–32): Jesus called Matthew (also known as Levi) away from his post as a tax collector and invites Matthew to follow him. After this call, Jesus joined Matthew for a meal attended by other tax collectors and sinners. It was scandalous for Jesus even to associate with such people. To share a meal — table fellowship — with sinners raised the eyebrows of the religious leaders. Jesus made it quite clear that he would share the company of sinners, not because he approved their actions, but because he had come to bring them healing and hope.

3. Passover (Exodus 12): At God's direction, Moses gave the Israelites explicit instructions for their final meal in Egypt. The meal, to be shared by families or groups of families, consisted of roasted lamb, unleavened bread, and bitter herbs. They were to eat the meal dressed for their escape from Egypt. The blood of the lamb that forms the centerpiece of the meal was dabbed on the doorposts and lintel of the Israelites' homes as a sign that the angel of death should pass over these homes when killing the firstborn. This meal, in ritualized form, is celebrated annually by the Jewish people in obedience to God's command.

2. Wedding Feast of the Lamb (Revelation 19:9–10): The Book of Revelation speaks briefly of the wedding feast of the Lamb to be celebrated in the new Jerusalem. Those who remain faithful to the end will be invited to share in this feast. This wedding feast of the Lamb is the heavenly banquet which is our desired end and in which the Eucharistic liturgy participates.

1. Last Supper (Matthew 26; Mark 14; Luke 22): The night before he died, Jesus gathered with his closest disciples and friends to share a final meal together. Knowing that his time on earth was drawing to a close, Jesus blessed and broke the bread and blessed and shared the wine. These were common actions at any meal. But what Jesus did was quite uncommon. In the form of bread and wine, Jesus gives his disciples his own Body and Blood and commands them to share this meal in his memory. Still today we follow this command as the faithful gather around the table to share in the Eucharist.

ANGELIC APPEARANCES

In the Bible, angels serve as messengers of God. They act as intermediaries between heaven and earth. They warn, guard, counsel, call, and support.

10. Angel in Eden (Genesis 3:1–24): After Adam and Eve are expelled from the Garden of Eden, God sends an angel — a cherubim to be exact — to stand guard over the entrance to the Garden and to prevent access to the tree of life, keeping Adam and Eve from an eternity of poor decisions.

9. Raphael with Tobiah (Tobit 5–12): In heaven, the archangel Raphael places prayers before God. Thus, he carried the prayers of Tobit and Sarah. In response to these prayers, God sent Raphael to earth to help them. Raphael accompanied Tobit's son, Tobiah, on his journey, finding a cure for Tobit's blindness and facilitating the successful marriage of Tobiah and Sarah. After the journey ended, Raphael revealed his true identity. He reminds us of the efficacy of prayer.

8. The Angels Who Visit Abraham (Genesis 18:1–15): When Abraham caught sight of three men traveling near his tent, he immediately invited them to rest in the shade and prepared a meal for them. In response to Abraham's generous hospitality, the three men revealed that Abraham and his wife Sarah will have a son, though they are elderly. It is only in the next chapter that the visitors are revealed as angels.

7. Michael (Revelation 12:7–12): The Book of Revelation recounts the military exploits of Michael, the archangel who leads the other angels in a battle against the dragon, Satan. He is the embodiment of the fight against evil, protecting human beings from the efforts of the Devil.

6. Annunciation to Zechariah (Luke 1:5–25): The archangel Gabriel appeared to Zechariah as he fulfilled his priestly duty offering incense in the Temple. Gabriel told Zechariah that he and his wife Elizabeth would have a son despite their advanced years. Gabriel gave instruction about how the child was to be raised, dedicated to the Lord and prepared for his prophetic mission. When Zechariah expressed doubt about the angel's message, Gabriel announced that he would be mute until the prediction was fulfilled by the birth of John the Baptist. Sometimes, it is good news that we doubt the most.

5. Call of Isaiah (Isaiah 6): Isaiah's call as a prophet is quite dramatic. He saw a vision of the enthroned Lord accompanied by six angels singing praise. When Isaiah expressed his unworthiness, one of the angels touched Isaiah's lips with an ember taken from the altar, purifying him for the prophetic mission which he accepts wholeheartedly.

4. Warnings to Joseph (Matthew 2:13–15 and 19–23): Twice, an angel of the Lord appeared to Joseph in dreams to warn him about danger. The first angel warned Joseph that Herod is plotting to kill Jesus, whom he sees as a threat to his throne. Because of the angel's warning,

Joseph escaped to Egypt with Jesus and Mary. In Egypt, they would be beyond Herod's reach. Later, another angel appeared to Joseph in a dream, informing him of Herod's death and warning that Herod's son was now in power. Because of this warning, the Holy Family moved from Egypt to Nazareth, from whence Jesus would begin his ministry.

3. Angel Saving Isaac (Genesis 22:1–19): God tested Abraham's faith by telling him to offer his beloved son, Isaac, as a burnt offering. Trusting in God, Abraham obeyed this command. As Abraham was about to kill Isaac, an angel called out to stop him. After Abraham offered a ram in his son's place, the angel spoke again, promising Abraham that his descendants would be countless because of his faith and obedience.

2. Annunciation to Joseph (Matthew 1:18–25): In the troubling days after Joseph found out that his betrothed, Mary, was pregnant, an angel appeared to him in a dream, reassuring him about marrying Mary. The angel explained that the child was conceived by the Holy Spirit and was destined to save human beings from sin. Once again, Joseph trusted in the angel's message and received Mary's child as his own.

1. Annunciation to Mary (Luke 1:26–38): At the beginning of his visit, Gabriel greeted Mary, informing her that she had found favor with God. He told her that she would conceive a child by the power of the Holy Spirit, so that her child would be the Son of God. Mary questioned how this could happen since she was a virgin, but she accepted Gabriel's assurances and embraced God's will for her, answering "Yes" to God's plan.

BATTLES OF THE BIBLE

There are many different kinds of battles in the Bible, ranging from full-scale military engagements to battles of wits.

10. Jael vs. Sisera (The Battle of the Jezreel Valley) (Judges 4): This first battle recounted in the Book of Judges is notable because victory for the Israelites comes from an unlikely source. Under the leadership of the general Barak, the Israelites had forced the Canaanite army and its general Sisera into retreat. But it was not the soldiers who killed Sisera. Jael, the wife of a Canaanite ally, double crossed him, inviting him to rest in her tent and killing him while he slept.

9. Sadducees vs. Pharisees (Acts 23): This battle is evidence of Paul's intelligence and quick thinking. He was brought before the Sanhedrin to be questioned about his teaching. Rather than go on the defensive, Paul used his opening statement to exploit the theological differences on the resurrection of the dead between the Saducees and the Pharisees. The argument between the Sanhedrin's factions became so heated that the soldiers took Paul back to prison lest he be injured in the fray.

8. Judah vs. Babylon (2 Kings 25): After the reign of Solomon, the military strength of Israel was on the downhill slope. As their fidelity to the covenant wavered, so did their political fate. The nation split between North and South (Israel and Judah), with the North falling to invasion. Despite numerous attempts at renewed fidelity to the covenant, Judah fell before the might of the Babylonian Empire. The Temple was destroyed, and the people were sent into exile.

7. Samson vs. Philistines (Judges 15–16): Samson is best known for his prodigious strength. God gave him this strength because he was dedicated to the Lord from his birth. His diet was strictly controlled, and he never cut his hair. As long as he was faithful to this vow, he remained strong. In his strength, he led the Israelites to many defeats of their perennial enemy, the Philistines. Tricked by Delilah into giving away his secret, Samson's hair was cut, and he was captured and blinded by the Philistines. But, Samson kept fighting to the death. Put on display before the Philistine leaders, Samson toppled the pillars of the building and killed the leaders.

6. The Israelites vs. the Amalekites (Exodus 17): The Israelites' journey from Egypt to the Promised Land was not without conflict. In the most famous battle, the Israelites faced off against the Amalekites. The Israelites were led by Joshua. Moses stood on a mountain overlooking the battlefield. As long as he held his staff over the field, the Israelites had the advantage in the battle. When Moses rested, the Israelites' fortunes waned. So, Aaron and Hur provided a rock for Moses to rest and, when his arms grew tired, they supported him. No battle is ever won without the right support.

5. David vs. Goliath (1 Samuel 17): The most famous battle in the Bible was also the most mismatched. A young shepherd armed with a slingshot took on a well-armored giant who made his living as a fighter. Goliath proved the old adage that the bigger they are, the harder they fall. He underestimated David's skill and commitment. David stunned Goliath with a well-slung stone and was able to behead him with his own sword, winning the day for the Israelites.

4. Elijah vs. the Prophets of Baal (1 Kings 18): In the most amusing battle in the Bible, Elijah faces off against the company of prophets of Baal. The subject of the battle: whose god is stronger? They set a task to see whose god will complete it most successfully. The prophets of Baal and Elijah will each prepare a bull as a burnt offering. The winner will be the god who consumes the burnt offering fastest. Despite the zealous efforts of the prophets of Baal (and the amusing taunts of Elijah), their god fails to rally to the cause. Of course, the Lord goes above and beyond, making it known that he is the one true God.

3. Israel vs. Jericho (Joshua 6): The Battle of Jericho is notable because one of the strongest cities in Canaan fell without a single shot. For six days, the Israelites marched around the city, following priests carrying the Ark of the Covenant. On the seventh day, they marched around the city seven times. Then, at a signal, the people made as much noise as they could — blowing horns and trumpets and shouting. Then, as the song says, the walls came tumbling down. This fortress city fell in a single day.

2. Jesus vs. Satan (Matthew 4, Mark 1, Luke 4): The Gospels recount an epic battle between Jesus and Satan in the desert. The devil tried to tempt Jesus away from his mission, offering him food, power, and riches. Jesus rejected these temptations. This battle involved no violence. Rather, Jesus and the devil faced off with their wits, trading Scripture texts in support of their positions. In the end, Satan retreated, but Luke lets us know that he will be back.

1. Good vs. Evil (entire Bible — see especially Revelation and Ephesians 6): In summary, the Bible is the story of the epic battle between good and evil. God has created human beings for good and for union with him. Satan entices human beings to trust in their own power and will rather than God. Trusting in one's one power over that of God is the root of all evil. Satan's path leads to death; God's path leads to life. In Jesus, the battle is won, once and for all. Death is vanquished. Through faith in Christ, we win.

TIMES GOD SHOWED MERCY AND FORGIVENESS

From the very beginning, human beings have sinned, choosing their own will over God's. Fortunately, God is always willing to forgive those who repent and strive to reform their lives.

10. Matthew (Matthew 9:9–13): Matthew was a tax collector. Tax collectors collaborated with the occupying Romans and were not noted for their honesty. They were viewed as public sinners. Despite all this baggage, Jesus called Matthew to be one of the Twelve, his closest companions. Even more, Jesus went to dinner in Matthew's home. When criticized, Jesus made it clear that he came to call sinners.

9. People of Israel during the Exodus (see especially Exodus 34): Despite the Lord's displays of power in bringing the Israelites out of slavery in Egypt, over the course of their forty-year wandering in the desert, the Israelites frequently failed to live up to the covenant that they made with God on Mount Sinai. Though God punished the Israelites, he showed mercy and remained faithful, keeping Israel as his people.

8. The Sinful Woman (Luke 7:36–50): While Jesus was at dinner at the home of Simon the Pharisee, a woman, known as a public sinner approached Jesus in tears. Her tears of repentance were so copious that they washed Jesus' feet. She proceeded to dry his feet with her hair and kiss them repeatedly. Her love and repentance were so overwhelming that Jesus forgave her sins and sent her on her way in peace.

7. Israel in Exile (see especially Isaiah and Jeremiah): Because of their infidelity, the people of Israel were carried into exile by the armies who conquered them. Though God knew this punishment was just, he sent his prophets among the people, offering them messages of comfort and hope.

6. The Woman Caught in Adultery (John 8:1–11): In an attempt to trap Jesus, the community leaders brought a woman caught in adultery before Jesus to see if he would condemn her to death, the punishment Moses decreed for adultery. Rather than fall into their trap, Jesus turned it back on them. He challenged the person without sin to be the first to throw a stone at her. Of course, the crowd drifted away. Jesus gave the woman her life and challenged her to avoid sin in the future. And no, Scripture never tells us what happened to the man involved.

5. Peter (see especially Matthew 26; Mark 14; Luke 22; and John 18 and 21): Having spent three years traveling with Jesus, listening to him preach and watching him perform miracles, in a time of crisis Peter denied even knowing Jesus — not once, but three times! Rather than risk his own safety, Peter betrayed his dear friend. Yet Jesus forgave him, and he remained the rock on which Jesus built his Church.

4. David (2 Samuel 11–12; Psalm 51): Attracted by her beauty, David committed adultery with Bathsheba, the wife of his general Uriah. When she became pregnant, David tried to hide his sin, inviting Uriah home for a conference. Due to the discipline of war, Uriah refused to spend a night of his visit with his wife. His plan having failed, David condemned Uriah to death in the fighting. Called to account for his sin by the prophet Nathan, David repented deeply, begging God's mercy. The beautiful Psalm 51 gives words to his plea. God heard his prayer and forgave David.

3. Adam and Eve (Genesis 3): Adam and Eve commit the first sin in the Bible, choosing to disobey God's command by eating the fruit of the tree from which they were forbidden to eat. Though God punished them, casting them out of Eden and making them subject to death, he showed mercy as well. In the fullness of time, he sent a Savior to destroy death forever.

2. Paul (Acts of the Apostles, especially chapters 7–9): When we first see Paul, then called Saul, he is complicit in the martyrdom of Stephen. Inspired by this violence, he became an enthusiastic persecutor of those who believe in Christ, even getting permission to travel to other cities to arrest Christians and bring them back to Jerusalem for trial. But God did not give up on him. Instead, after a personal encounter with the risen Christ, Paul got a second chance, reformed his life, and preached the Gospel throughout the known world until he suffered a martyr's death.

1. The Soldiers at the Crucifixion (Luke 23:34): The soldiers were just following orders — crucifying another condemned criminal. In the midst of the violence and pain, Jesus asked his Father to forgive them in the most haunting words of Scripture, "Father, forgive them, they know not what they do."

CITIES OF BLINDING LIGHTS (WELL, NOT REALLY)

The Bible speaks of God's relationship with his people. God acts in our world, in the midst of our existence, in the quiet of the desert and the bustle of the city.

10. Ephesus: Ephesus was an important city in Asia Minor (in what is now Turkey). Paul visited this city on his second and third missionary journeys. In later years, Ephesus became closely associated with the Blessed Virgin Mary.

9. Capernaum: Capernaum was a town on the shores of the Sea of Galilee. As such, it was the home to many fishermen and others who made a living on the sea. Peter lived in Capernaum, and Jesus used it as a home base for his ministry. Jesus visited Capernaum frequently in the course of his ministry, preaching there and performing miracles.

8. Athens: Though Greece was no longer a great world power, Athens remained a center of learning, culture, and religious practice. While in Athens, Paul debated with philosophers and gave an important speech at the Areopagus, introducing those who worshipped other gods to Jesus Christ.

7. Emmaus: Emmaus was a town not far from Jerusalem. It does not seem to have been an important town. In the Bible, it is noted for one thing: it was the destination of two disciples travelling on the afternoon after Jesus rose from the dead. In the course of their journey, Jesus began to walk with them, talking with them and explaining the Scriptures to him. The disciples invited Jesus to stay with them in Emmaus, and they recognized him in the breaking of the bread.

6. Antioch: Antioch was an important city in the Middle East and an early center of Christianity. In fact, it was in Antioch that Jesus' followers first received the name "Christians." Antioch remained an important city throughout the first centuries of the Church's history.

5. Damascus: Damascus is the oldest continuously inhabited city in the world. Paul was on his way to Damascus to arrest the Christians there when he heard Jesus asking why Paul was persecuting him. After this encounter, Paul was struck blind and had to be led to Damascus. In Damascus, he regained his sight and began the mission that would encompass the rest of his life: preaching Christ.

4. Nazareth: Nazareth was a small town in Galilee, remarkable only because the Holy Family of Jesus, Mary, and Joseph made their home there. Throughout his ministry, Jesus was known as a Nazorean, surprising to many people who did not expect a great prophet, let alone the Messiah, to come from Nazareth.

3. Bethlehem: The word Bethlehem means "house of bread." This small town, not far from Jerusalem, was the hereditary home of the family of King David. As a descendant of the House of David, Joseph traveled to Bethlehem for the census, along with Mary, his wife. While in Bethlehem, she gave birth to her firstborn son, Jesus.

2. Rome: Rome was the principal city of an Empire that controlled much of the known world. It was the center of political and military power. The Acts of the Apostles concludes with Paul teaching and preaching while under arrest in Rome. It was the place where Peter and Paul were martyred for the faith. Rome became and remains the center of the Church.

1. Jerusalem: No other city is as central to the Bible as the city of Jerusalem. Jerusalem became the capital of Israel in the reign of King David. Rebuilding Jerusalem and its Temple after the exile was an important step in the restoration of the nation. Jerusalem remains central in the New Testament. Jesus often preached in the Temple. He entered the city in triumph, and he was put to death just outside the city. The Apostles went out from Jerusalem to preach the risen Christ. The Book of Revelation sees heaven as the new Jerusalem — a perfect city with God at its center, where all the faithful will dwell forever.

ON THE MOUNTAINTOP

In the Bible, mountains are places to pray alone or to encounter God.

10. Mountains of Ararat (Genesis 8): As the waters of the Flood receded, the tops of mountains were the first land to emerge from the water. The ark came to rest on the mountains of Ararat with Noah and his family inside. From there, Moses released the dove to see when the waters had receded enough so that he could emerge from the ark and begin to rebuild his life.

9. Mount Hermon (Matthew 16): Mount Hermon was the northernmost part of the Promised Land. In Old Testament times, it was associated with the worship of Baal. In New Testament times, the town of Caesarea Philippi was at its base. At Caesarea Philippi, Peter made his confession that Jesus was the Messiah and the Son of God.

8. Moriah (Genesis 22): God told Abraham to travel to the land of Moriah and to sacrifice his son Isaac on a mountain there. Trusting in God, Abraham followed God's command. Seeing his faith, God sent an angel to stay Abraham's hand before he could kill Isaac. Instead, Abraham offered a ram as a sacrifice in place of Isaac. God praised Abraham for his faith and promised that his descendants will be numerous.

7. Mount Nebo (Deuteronomy 34; 2 Maccabees 2): God had told Moses that he would not set foot in the Promised Land. However, God did grant him a glimpse of the Promised Land from the heights of Mount Nebo. According to the Second Book of Maccabees, at the time of the Exile, the prophet Jeremiah hid the Ark of the Covenant in a cave on Mount Nebo to protect it from the invaders.

6. Mount Tabor (Matthew 17; Mark 9: Luke 9): Mount Tabor is generally regarded as the location of Jesus' Transfiguration. Jesus took Peter, James, and John up the mountain with him. While they were there, Jesus was transfigured, appearing to them in all his glory and conversing with Moses and Elijah, symbols of the Law and the Prophets.

5. Mount Gerizim (John 4): Mount Gerizim is the principal mountain in Samaria. For Samaritans, Mount Gerizim, not Jerusalem, is the place God designated for his worship. But Jesus explains to the woman at the well that the *place* of worship is not important. Rather, what is essential is that we worship God "in Spirit and truth" (John 4:24).

4. Mount Carmel (1 Kings 18): Mount Carmel is the scene of the battle between the prophet Elijah and the prophets of Baal. Here God shows his power is greater than that of Baal, causing Baal's prophets to recognize that the Lord is God.

3. Mount of Olives (also called Mount Olivet): The Mount of Olives is located very near Jerusalem. Jesus often met there with his disciples to teach them. According to the Gospel of Matthew, Jesus and his disciples went to the Mount of Olives after the Last Supper. The Garden of Gethsemane rests at the base of the mountain. According to the first chapter of the Acts of the Apostles, Jesus' Ascension to heaven took place from the Mount of Olives.

2. Mount Sinai (Exodus; 1 Kings 19): Also called Mount Horeb, Sinai is the mountain of Moses' encounter with God. It is on Mount Sinai that Moses sees the burning bush and there that he receives the Laws of the covenant. Later, Elijah journeys to Sinai — a trip of forty days and forty nights — where he encounters God.

1. Mount Zion: Jerusalem is built on a hill, and the Temple is on a hill atop the city. The biblical phrase "going up to the Temple" is to be taken literally. Going to the Temple meant climbing the steep hill to the entrance. In Isaiah and Hebrews, Mount Zion is used to refer to the heavenly Jerusalem as well — the place where the faithful will dwell with God forever.

WATER, WATER EVERYWHERE!

Water provides transportation, irrigation, and occupation. In arid landscapes, access to a body of water means life. It is not surprising that water plays an important role in the Bible.

10. Waters of the Firmament (Genesis 1): The Creation Story in Genesis 1 describes the waters of the firmament. On the second day of creation, God creates a dome that divides the waters. The waters above the dome become part of the sky. On the third day, the waters below the dome are gathered into the sea, allowing dry land to appear. From the very beginning, water has been essential to human life.

9. Nile River: The Nile was and is the principal river of Egypt. Moses' mother hid him along the banks of the river to protect him from the Pharaoh's edict to kill all the male children born of Hebrew women. In the first plague, God turns the water of the Nile into blood, rendering it undrinkable and threatening the very survival of Egypt. In the second plague, the Nile teemed with frogs. These first two plagues attacked the heart of Egyptian life — yet Pharaoh hardened his heart.

8. Red Sea (Exodus 14): The Red Sea lay between Egypt and the wilderness that led to the Promised Land. As the Israelites made their escape from slavery in Egypt, they were caught between the Red Sea and the pursuing Egyptian army. To save his chosen people, God parted the waters of the Red Sea so that the Israelites could pass through it on dry land. After the Israelites passed through, God let the waters flow back, drowning Pharaoh's entire army and allowing the people of Israel safe passage to Mount Sinai.

7. Water Flowing from the Temple (Ezekiel 47): An angel shows the prophet Ezekiel a vision of water flowing from the Temple. This water, which deepens as Ezekiel watches, is a source of life and healing. The water forms a river that abounds with fish and nourishes animals. It makes fresh any sea it touches, and the trees on its banks produce fruit and medicine.

6. Rivers of Babylon (Psalm 137): The Babylonian Empire was located near two great rivers, the Tigris and the Euphrates. After the fall of Jerusalem, all except the poorest Israelites were exiled to Babylon. In Psalm 137, an exiled psalmist speaks of sitting beside the rivers, refusing to sing the sacred songs of Israel for the entertainment of their captors.

5. Jordan River: The Jordan River flows from the Sea of Galilee to the Dead Sea — from Galilee to Judea. The Jordan was the primary location for the ministry of John the Baptist. He preached along the banks of the Jordan and those moved to repentance by his words were baptized in the river. Jesus came to the Jordan, seeking baptism from John. The Spirit descended on Jesus in the form of a dove, and God proclaimed that Jesus was his beloved Son.

4. Sea of Galilee: Known by several names, including the Sea of Tiberias, Lake Gennesaret, and Lake Kinnarot, this body of water is a central location in Jesus' ministry. Before being called, at least four of Jesus' Apostles made their living as fishermen on the sea. During his public ministry, Jesus regularly traveled around and across the sea. He calmed a storm on the sea and walked across its surface. After his Resurrection, Jesus appeared to some of his disciples there. The Sea of Galilee was a place of preaching and miracles.

3. Mediterranean Sea: The Mediterranean Sea was the largest body of water in the Ancient Near East. It was essential to trade, and many cities developed along its shores. In addition, the Mediterranean Sea was an important artery of travel. Paul sailed the Mediterranean on his missionary journeys. Unfortunately for Paul, however, his travel on the Mediterranean often ended badly — with three shipwrecks.

2. Pool of Fire (Revelation 19–21): The Book of Revelation describes the fate of the unfaithful as well as the faithful. While the faithful will dwell with God in the heavenly Jerusalem, those whose names are not in the Book of Life — those who were not faithful to God on earth — will be cast into a pool of fire where they will suffer an everlasting death.

1. River of Life-Giving Water (Revelation 7 and 22): The Book of Revelation describes the heavenly Jerusalem where those who are faithful to the end will dwell with God forever. The city is watered by a river of life-giving water which flows from the throne of the Lamb. This water bears grace and life to those who will live forever.

THREE

SAYINGS AND SUCH

FAMOUS SAYINGS

Many people have a favorite Bible passage that gives comfort or inspires. The texts that follow are among the best known passages in the Bible. These sayings are marked by the poetry of their words and by the deep meaning they bear.

10. "Ask and it will be given to you; seek and you will find; knock and the door will be opened to you." (Matthew 7:7): This verse underlies the fervent belief in the power of prayer. As God's precious children, we turn to our loving Father, asking for what we need and trusting that he will give us all good things.

9. "The LORD gave and the LORD has taken away; / blessed be the name of the LORD!" (Job 1:21): Despite the misfortunes that befall him, Job makes this statement of faith in God's providence. No human life will ever be without misfortune, even tragedy in some cases. However, even in our darkest times, God will be with us, sharing our burdens.

8. "So faith, hope, love remain, these three; but the greatest of these is love." (1 Corinthians 13:13): This verse concludes the famous description of love found in the thirteenth chapter of the First Letter of Saint Paul to the Corinthians ("Love is patient …"). This verse reminds us that much of what people seek — fame, money, power — does not last. Eventually, all of those things will fade away.

In the end, only faith, hope, and love remain. They are the gifts to be valued.

7. "God saw that it was good." (Genesis 1:10): As God engages in the work of creation, he finds the things he has made to be good. (When it comes to human beings, he finds his work "very good.") The created world is not some evil we must survive in order to enjoy heaven. It is good — a gift of God — in itself. Creation in general and human life in particular should be nurtured, protected, and valued.

6. "Come after me, and I will make you fishers of men." (Matthew 4:19): With these words, Jesus called four fishermen to be his disciples. Scripture recounts that Peter, Andrew, James, and John abandoned their livelihoods and followed Jesus immediately. The power of their faith, evidenced in their preaching and their works, would help to build the Church.

5. "May it be done to me according to your word." (Luke 1:38): When the angel Gabriel told Mary that she would bear a child who would be the Son of God, she had to be startled and disturbed by his words. But her response in this famous saying is a model for all the faithful. We should choose to accept God's will and follow his plan for us, even if it is hard to understand.

4. "Jesus Christ is the same yesterday, today, and forever." (Hebrews 13:8): This famous saying was the theme for the Jubilee Year 2000. Though times and people and political structures change, Jesus never does. He became human to share our hardships, and he opened the gates of heaven for us. Through it all, he is the unchanging God who desires what is best for all people.

3. "I am the way and the truth and the life." (John 14:6): If we seek to find our path in life, we can do no better than to follow Jesus, who will lead us to everlasting life. He is the source of all life and truth and the path that leads to God.

2. "Hear, O Israel! The LORD is our God, the LORD alone! Therefore, you shall love the LORD, your God, with your whole heart, and with your whole being, and with your whole strength." (Deuteronomy 6:4–5): These verses, known in Hebrew as the *Shema*, form the foundational prayer of Judaism, attesting to belief in the one true God who deserves all our love. These words should be on our lips and in our hearts morning, noon, and night.

1. "Do to others whatever you would have them do to you." (Matthew 7:12): Known simply as the Golden Rule, this verse is likely the best-known Bible text. Even people who profess no religion have heard of it. The message is quite simple to understand, though quite challenging to carry out. We must treat everyone we encounter as we would wish to be treated — with love, with respect, with dignity.

PARABLES: THE BEST STORIES EVER TOLD

Jesus often taught the crowds using stories. These stories used situations familiar to the listeners to teach important truths. In some cases, Jesus explained the meaning of the parable to his disciples later. In other cases, the meaning would have been clear and challenging to all who heard. Even today, these parables remain among the favorite and most familiar portions of Scripture.

10. Parable of the Talents (Matthew 25:14–30; Luke 19:11–27): Jesus told a story about a wealthy man who goes on a journey, leaving money with his servants to invest during his absence. Two of these servants used the money well, earning their master a good return. The master commends and rewards their industriousness. The third servant, fearing his master's displeasure in the event of a loss, hides the money away to safeguard it. The master responds to this course of action with anger, dismissing the servant and giving his money to the man who produced the best return. With this vivid story, Jesus reminds us that we are expected to use our gifts well, putting them at the service of the community.

9. Parable of the Virgins (Matthew 25:1–13): Jesus tells of ten virgins who are invited to accompany a bridegroom to the wedding celebration. Five of the virgins come prepared with extra oil for their lamps while the others, foolishly, do not. When the bridegroom is delayed, the lamps begin to go out. The virgins who did not bring extra oil are forced to go off to find a merchant who can sell them more oil. During their absence, the bridegroom arrives and the celebration begins. When the foolish virgins return, presumably well supplied with oil, they are not admitted to the celebration. We need to be prepared to meet Jesus, whenever he comes. Jesus will come on his schedule, not ours, and we must be ready always.

8. Parable of the Dishonest Steward (Luke 16:1–8): A man discovers that his steward has been dishonest and, quite understandably, decides to dismiss him. The steward is ordered to organize the accounts for the transition. The steward realizes that he is unlikely to find new employment as a steward. Who would trust a man dismissed for dishonesty? The other employment options — manual labor and begging — hold no appeal. So, the steward invites his master's debtors to write new promissory notes, deducting his commission. The debtors now owe him favors that he can collect while he looks for new work. The master commends this shrewdness. Jesus reminds his listeners to use their worldly goods well, but to remember that wealth in this world will not necessarily lead to happiness in the next.

7. Parable of the Rich Man and Lazarus (Luke 16:19–31): In this parable, most unusually, the rich man goes unnamed while the beggar's name is known. Jesus contrasts the life of a man of great wealth who enjoys every luxury with the life of the beggar Lazarus who lies at his gate. Lazarus is poor, hungry, and ill. He does not have the strength to shoo away the dogs that lick the sores on his body. In time, both men die. The rich man descends to the fiery netherworld while Lazarus rests in the bosom of Abraham. When the rich man begs Abraham to send Lazarus to cool his tongue, Abraham notes that the fortunes of Lazarus and the rich man are now reversed. Even more, people cannot pass from the bosom of Abraham to the netherworld. The rich man then asks that Lazarus be sent to warn his brothers so that they will not share his fate. Abraham refuses, noting that those who ignore the teachings of the Law and the Prophets will not listen to anyone, even someone who comes back from the dead. This parable illustrates Jesus' particular concern for the poor and vulnerable, a concern his followers are called to emulate.

6. Parable of the Pharisee and the Tax Collector (Luke 18:9–14): Jesus recounts the prayers of two men — one an upstanding member of the community — a Pharisee — and the other an outcast and presumed sinner — a tax collector. The Pharisee uses his prayer to remind God of his own righteousness and worthiness. The tax collector begs God's mercy. Jesus makes it very clear which prayer God will receive with greater joy and, in so doing, teaches us how to approach God in prayer.

5. Parable of the Sower (Matthew 13:1–9; Mark 4:1–9; Luke 8:4–8): Jesus uses a common agricultural image to explain varying receptions of the word of God. As the sower sows seed, it falls in various places — on the path, in the rocks, among thorns, and on good soil. The yield of the seed is decided by where it falls. Only the seed that falls on the good soil will yield fruit. As Jesus explains the parable, the seed represents the word of God. In some people, the word is stolen from them by Satan before it takes root. For others, the word is received with joy at first but, because its roots are shallow, the joy fades quickly. Yet another group allows the word to be crowded out by other cares and concerns. But those who let the word take root in their hearts bear great fruit.

4. Parable of the Workers in the Vineyard (Matthew 20:1–16): Jesus tells of a vineyard owner who goes out at varying times of the day to hire workers for his vineyard, promising to pay them what is fair. Some laborers put in a full day's work while others work but a few hours. When the time comes to pay the workers, the owner gives each man a full day's pay. The workers who spent the day in the vineyard are angry that they did not receive more than those who worked only a few hours. The vineyard owner points out that he has not cheated anyone. The workers who worked all day received a fair wage. The owner has chosen to be generous with those who worked less. Jesus reminds us that God's generous love is available to all, no matter how late we come to him.

3. Parable of the Good Samaritan (Luke 10:29–37): Jesus told of a traveler attacked by robbers while going from Jerusalem to Jericho. Left by the side of the road to die, the man was passed by a priest and a Levite. We don't know why they walked by him. They may have been afraid the robbers were still nearby or they may not have wanted to get involved. However, when a Samaritan came across the man, he treated his wounds and transported him to an inn for further care, assuming responsibility for payment. Jews considered Samaritans to be religious outcasts. Making a Samaritan the hero of the story — the one who acted with mercy and compassion — was a shocking twist. Jesus told his listeners that being neighbor was not a matter of national or religious alliance, but of love.

2. Parable of the Sheep and the Goats (Matthew 25:31–46): This parable describes the last judgment. It presents Jesus as a king who sorts out his people the way a shepherd separates sheep from goats. The first group is invited to enter the heavenly kingdom. When they ask why they have been chosen to enter the kingdom, the king commends them for caring for him when he was naked, hungry, in prison, and ill. The second group is sent to eternal punishment because they ignored the king when he was in need. Neither group can recall seeing the king in need. The king explains that any kindness done for one of the least ones was done for him. Similarly, ignoring the needs of the least ones means ignoring the needs of the king. We will be judged by how we care for those around us, regardless of their status.

1. Parable of the Prodigal Son (Luke 15:11–32): A son demands that his father give him the portion of the inheritance that will come to him and leaves his family home to live a life of indulgence — until the money runs out. Out of money in a foreign land during a famine, the son takes a menial job that barely keeps him alive. Coming to his senses, the son decides to return home. He does not expect to resume his former status. He is willing to become a servant. The father welcomes him back with great love and joy — as if he had come back from the dead. The older brother did not receive his brother back with similar joy, resenting his father's forgiveness, seeing it as an insult. The father reaffirms his love for his elder son, but does not back off from his forgiveness of the younger son. In this parable, Jesus reminds us that God's forgiveness is always available to those who seek it.

PROMISES, PROMISES

God always wants what is best for us, offering us strength and comfort according to our needs. Many passages in the Bible offer us that comfort and convey God's promise to be with us always.

10. "For I know well the plans I have in mind for you — oracle of the Lord — plans for your welfare and not for woe, so as to give you a future of hope." (Jeremiah 29:11): This passage from the Book of the Prophet Jeremiah reminds the Israelites in exile — and us — that, even if we do not understand them, God's plans for us are always for the best.

9. "Can a mother forget her infant, / be without tenderness for the child of her womb? / Even should she forget, / I will never forget you. / See, upon the palms of my hands I have engraved you." (Isaiah 49:14–16a): No matter what, we are always in God's heart, engraved on the palm of his hand so we are always close to him. Even if those closest to us abandon us, God will not.

8. "They that hope in the Lord will renew their strength, / they will soar on eagles' wings; / They will run and not grow weary, / walk and not grow faint." (Isaiah 40:31): When our minds and bodies fail, God is our support. When we cannot go on, God carries us through.

7. "I heard a loud voice from the throne saying, 'Behold, God's dwelling is with the human race. He will dwell with them and they will be his people and God himself will always be with them [as their God]. He will wipe every tear from their eyes, and there shall be no more death or mourning, wailing or pain, [for] the old order has passed away.'" (Revelation 21:3–4): The Book of Revelation provides a vision of heaven, where the faithful will dwell with God forever. In heaven, we will be in God's direct presence where death and its effects no longer hold sway.

6. "For God so loved the world that he gave his only Son, so that everyone who believes in him might not perish but might have eternal life. For God did not send his Son into the world to condemn the world, but that the world might be saved through him." (John 3:16–17): This passage, often seen on posters at sporting events, reminds us that we are so precious to God that he was willing to sacrifice his Son to destroy death so that we could live forever.

5. "And the Word became flesh / and made his dwelling among us." (John 1:14): One of Scripture's greatest comforts is the realization that Jesus became human like us. Since Jesus shared the human experience, we can bring our difficulties and troubles to him and he will understand.

4. "Amen, I say to you, today you will be with me in Paradise." (Luke 23:43): Jesus spoke these words to the man crucified alongside him. Though the man was a criminal, he accepted the consequences of his actions and asked Jesus for forgiveness. No matter how great our sin and our distance from God, Jesus is always willing to welcome us back.

3. "Do not let your hearts be troubled. You have faith in God; have faith also in me." (John 14:1): Life is filled with stress and anxiety. We can always worry about something. Jesus reminds us that, if we have faith in him, we need not fear the troubles of this world.

2. "The LORD is my shepherd; / there is nothing I lack." (Psalm 23:1): This first line of the best known of all the Psalms reminds us that God will provide for all our needs. He will always be present to guide and protect us.

1. "And behold, I am with you always, until the end of the age." (Matthew 28:20): This closing line of Matthew's Gospel is Jesus' promise to always be with us. No matter what happens, Jesus is always present with us, in our joys and sorrows, successes and failures, hope and pain.

CHALLENGES

The words of Scripture instruct and inspire, exhort and comfort. Scripture also challenges us, calling us to conform our lives to Christ, living in selfless love.

10. "Sanctify Christ as Lord in your hearts. Always be ready to give an explanation to anyone who asks you for a reason for your hope." (1 Peter 3:15): Those who believe must always be willing to discuss their faith. This requirement means that we must continue to grow in our faith so that we will have the words we need when questioned by others.

9. "Go into the whole world and proclaim the gospel to every creature." (Mark 16:15): Through Baptism, Christians are called to evangelize — to proclaim the Gospel through their words and actions.

8. "Therefore I tell you, do not worry about your life and what you will eat, or about your body and what you will wear." (Luke 12:22): For many people, this verse is a great challenge. In today's society, we are bombarded with messages about food and clothing and health. With the addition of finances and work, life can become a mass of anxieties. Jesus challenges us to move beyond our anxieties and to place our trust in God.

7. "If you forgive others their transgressions, your heavenly Father will forgive you. But if you do not forgive others, neither will your Father forgive your transgressions." (Matthew 6:14–15): Forgiving those who have hurt us is a great challenge. It means letting go of our pain and our defensiveness, opening ourselves to the possibility of being hurt once again.

6. "Whoever wishes to be great among you will be your servant; whoever wishes to be first among you will be the slave of all." (Mark 10:43–44): Jesus made it clear to his disciples that his kingdom was about service, not power. Placing ourselves at the service of others and considering ourselves last is countercultural in a world that promotes personal achievement and status. But we are planning not for this world, but for the next.

5. "Go, sell what you have, and give to [the] poor and you will have treasure in heaven; then come, follow me." (Mark 10:21): This passage challenges on two levels. First, it requires that the Christian detach completely from the things we own and the things that own us. Second, it requires that we orient our lives to care for and service of the poor.

4. "Whoever wishes to come after me must deny himself, take up his cross, and follow me." (Mark 8:34): Every life has crosses — the burdens that we carry day after day. These burdens might be illness, concern about a loved one, job difficulties, or past hurts. Embracing these crosses and uniting our struggles to the suffering of Christ is the hallmark of a Christian life.

3. "So be perfect, just as your heavenly Father is perfect." (Matthew 5:48): Well, this is a high standard! Be as perfect as God! Obviously, human beings are imperfect and sinful. We are not God's equals. But we can strive each day to live as God would have us live, to follow in his path of righteousness and mercy.

2. "My Father, if it is possible, let this cup pass from me; yet, not as I will, but as you will." (Matthew 26:39, cf. Mark 14:36 and Luke 22:42): As disciples of Christ, we must follow his example, accepting God's will for us. As we grow in faith, we strive to conform our will to God's will ever more closely.

1. "I give you a new commandment: love one another. As I have loved you, so you also should love one another." (John 13:34): The standard of love by which we will be measured is that of Jesus' love for us. Jesus loved us so much that he laid down his life for us. We may never be at risk of dying for our brothers and sisters, but we will have to die to self to live more fully in Christ's love.

SYMBOLS, NOT CYMBALS
(THAT'S A DIFFERENT LIST)

The Bible often uses symbols to describe deeper realities, to illustrate important principles, and to foretell what may happen in the future. These symbols remain in the mind and help us to recall the actions of God in our lives.

10. The Exile's Bag (Ezekiel 12): God used Ezekiel the prophet to call the Hebrew people back to fidelity to the covenant, warning them of the consequences for infidelity. Ezekiel demonstrated one of those consequences, packing an exile's bag and leaving the city under the cover of darkness. He provided a visual reminder to people that, if they were not faithful to the Lord and his covenant, they would be cast out of the land.

9. Gold Tested in Fire (1 Peter 1): Gold tested in fire is used as a symbol for the faith of a believer, particularly one facing persecution. Gold is refined by heating it in fire in order to remove the impurities. In the same way, a believer is tested to remove sin and doubt, leaving only the precious gift of faith.

8. The Loincloth (Jeremiah 13): At the Lord's command, Jeremiah used a loincloth as a symbol of Judah (land controlled by two of the tribes of Israel). Jeremiah wore the loincloth for a period, and then he hid it behind a rock. Of course, when he checked on it later, the loincloth had rotted. God keeps his people close to them, as a loincloth is close to its wearer. When we are parted from God, immersed in our own pride, rot sets in.

7. The Golden Calf (Exodus 32): During the Israelites' sojourn in the desert, Moses was apart from the people for an extended period, conversing with God and learning of the covenant. The people grew anxious, fearing that Moses was dead. They pressured Aaron into melting down their jewelry to form an idol that they could worship as their God. A Golden Calf was the resulting idol. Though they had seen the power of God, they doubted him and his servant Moses. The Golden Calf has come to symbolize lack of faith.

6. A Scroll to Eat (Ezekiel 2–3, Revelation 10): Ezekiel and John (in Revelation) are invited by an angel to eat a scroll. The scroll symbolizes the word of God: the word Ezekiel was called to proclaim and the word that foretold the fate of the churches in Revelation. In both cases, the scroll tastes sweet, as the word of God is always sweet to the believer. But, in Revelation, the scroll later nauseates the one who eats it, turning his stomach sour, because it tells of the sufferings that the faithful will have to endure.

5. The Yoke (Jeremiah 28 and Matthew 11): A yoke is a bar that goes across the shoulders. It may be used to help pull a load, such as a wagon or a plow, or to carry a heavy load by distributing it more evenly. It could also be a symbol of servitude. In the time of Jeremiah, false prophets were preaching what people wanted to hear (which certainly made them popular). They announced that the yoke of Israel's conquerors would be broken. Jeremiah, speaking the truth given him by the Lord, was far less popular when he preached that the conqueror's wooden yoke would, indeed, be broken, only to be replaced by an unbreakable iron yoke. Later, Jesus reassured his followers that his "yoke is easy" and his "burden light" (Matthew 11:30). Serving Jesus is not a question of slavery, but a free giving of self in love.

4. The Four Creatures (Ezekiel 1, Revelation 4): Four creatures appear in both Ezekiel and Revelation. In Ezekiel, the creatures have four faces that resemble well-known creatures: a calf, a lion, a human being, and an eagle. In Revelation, the creatures resemble a calf, a lion, a human being, and an eagle. In the early years of the Church, those four creatures became symbols of the four Gospels. The human being is the symbol of Matthew since his Gospel begins with the genealogy. The lion is the symbol of Mark since, like the lion, Jesus emerges from the desert at the beginning of Mark's Gospel. The calf is the symbol of Luke since the Gospel of Luke begins with Zechariah offering sacrifice on the altar of the Temple (calves were frequently the animal of sacrifice). The eagle is the symbol of John, whose Gospel begins with a poetic prologue, announcing Jesus' pre-existence and unity with the God of all creation.

3. The Bow in the Clouds (Genesis 9): Noah and his family emerged from the ark after the flood had receded, and they offered a sacrifice of praise to God. God set a bow in the clouds as a sign of his covenant with Noah, promising that he will never again destroy all life on the planet. The bow is a symbol of God's boundless mercy and fidelity.

2. The Burning Bush (Exodus 3): A bush is aflame yet is not consumed. Unsurprisingly, the sight captures Moses' attention, and he approaches to investigate. The burning bush is a symbol of the presence of God, hallowing the place where

Moses stands. The voice of God came from the bush, calling Moses to accept the mission of liberating the people of Israel from slavery in Egypt.

1. The Cloud of Presence (Exodus 13–14, 19, and 33 and 1 Kings 8): Throughout the Exodus, God's presence with his people is symbolized by a pillar of cloud or of fire, leading the people and protecting them from enemies. Later in the journey, the cloud settles over the tent where Moses goes to meet with the Lord. Once Solomon has built the Temple in Jerusalem, a cloud overshadows the building, showing that God is dwelling with his people.

ALL GOOD GIFTS

Who doesn't like to receive gifts? This top ten list is a bit different from the rest. Though it has ten items, the top three are all tied for first. After all, when a gift is priceless, how can you rank it? (They are presented in reverse alphabetical order.)

10. The Staff of Moses (Exodus 7): A staff was not an unusual accessory for a shepherd like Moses. However, God's gift made his staff quite extraordinary. It was through this staff that God's power flowed. It humbled the staffs of the Egyptian magicians and produced the plagues. It parted the Red Sea and drew water from the rock.

9. Tithes (Genesis 14; Malachi 3; Luke 18): Tithes are our return to God in gratitude for all that he has given us. The first gifts given back to God come from Cain and Abel. However, tithes take a clearer form when Abraham gives a tenth of his plunder to the priest Melchizedek. However, by the time of Malachi, people are withholding their tithes. Rather than returning their gifts to God in gratitude, they hold back to ensure their comfort. However, in the Gospel of Luke, Jesus makes it clear that paying tithes is not enough in itself if the tithes do not come from a repentant and humble heart.

8. The Land of Israel (Genesis 12 and Exodus 3): God gives the land of Israel to Abraham and his descendants. He confirms this promise to Moses when he calls him to lead the people out of Egypt. Their destination will be the Promised Land — the land promised to Abraham. Throughout the Old Testament, the people's prosperity and security on the land is closely tied to their fidelity to the covenant.

7. Gold, Frankincense, and Myrrh (Matthew 2): Perhaps the most famous baby gifts ever! Gold was a traditional gift given to a king, representing worldly power and wealth. Frankincense is a gift for a priest. When burned, this sweet-smelling incense spirals up to the sky, as our prayers ascend to God. Myrrh is a more confusing gift. Though it smells wonderful and can be used as incense, in biblical times it was used to anoint a body for burial — a most unusual gift for a small child, but not for a baby king who came to lay down his life for all.

6. Money Placed at the Apostles' Feet (Acts 2:42–47 and 4:32–37): Twice, the Acts of the Apostles speaks of the generosity and communal care shown by the early Christians. Christians would place money at the feet of the Apostles to be shared with those who had little. Those who owned property sold it and gave the proceeds of the sale to the Apostles in a like manner. In this way, those with much provided for those who had little.

5. Wisdom (Proverbs, Wisdom, and Sirach): In the Books of Proverbs, Wisdom, and Sirach (the Wisdom of Ben Sira), the greatest gift for which anyone can hope is the gift of Wisdom. In fact, these texts are guidebooks teaching the seeker how to find Wisdom. For true Wisdom leads one, inevitably, to God.

4. A Child (see, for example, Genesis 18, Judges 13, 1 Samuel 1, and Luke 1): Praying to God for the gift of a child is a biblical custom that has stayed with us to this day. Isaac, Samson, Samuel, and John the Baptist are some of the children that Scripture presents as gifts from God to the faithful parents. Of course, the lack of a child is certainly not a sign of a lack of faith. Scripture reminds us that a child is not a parent's right, but a gift of God.

3. The Holy Spirit (see especially John 14–17): On the night before he died, Jesus announced two gifts. Both of these gifts ensured that he would remain with us, even after his Ascension. The gift of the Spirit brings comfort, gives hope, opens our minds and hearts to understand Christ's teaching, and strengthens us to carry out the mission of the Church. The Spirit came in fullness after the Resurrection.

2. Eucharist (Matthew 26; Mark 14; Luke 22; John 6): The second gift Jesus announced before his death was the gift of the Eucharist. At the Last Supper, gathered with those he loved, he gave them the gift of his Body and Blood under the appearances of bread and wine. This bread is the Bread of Life that comes from heaven and will lead us to eternal life. Through the Eucharist, Jesus will remain present with us always until we share in the heavenly banquet.

1. Eternal Life (Gospels): God destined man and woman for eternal life in union with him. However, one of the effects of the first sin was to make human beings subject to death, closing the gates of heaven. By the death and Resurrection of Jesus, death is conquered and the gates of heaven are opened once again. Because Jesus died in atonement for our sins, we can live forever with God in heaven.

PUNISHMENTS

God gave human beings the gift of free will. Unfortunately, human beings sometimes use that gift to choose sin and evil rather than the good. The Bible tells many stories about these poor choices and the punishments that follow.

10. Being Eaten by Bears (2 Kings 2:23–24): As the prophet Elisha traveled from Jericho to Bethel, a group of children teased him about his baldness and tried to chase him away. Forty-two of the children were eaten by two bears that came out of the woods. One may assume that the other children in town learned an important lesson about respecting prophets and not bullying.

9. Snow White Scales (Numbers 12:1–15): Aaron and Miriam grew jealous of Moses' role as God's spokesman to the people of Israel. God reproved them for their envy and highlighted his unique relationship with Moses. As punishment, Miriam was stricken with a skin disease, leaving her covered in white scales. In accord with the law, she had to live outside the camp until her disease passed. Out of respect for Miriam and her brothers, the people did not break camp until she was healed.

8. Herem (1 Samuel 15): *Herem*, also called the ban, is a punishment inflicted on the losing side in a battle. If the ban was imposed, the soldiers were not permitted to take captives or plunder from the conquered city. The captured people were killed, and all material goods were destroyed. In this most devastating form of warfare, nothing is left alive.

7. Pillar of Salt (Genesis 19:15–26): God condemned the cities of Sodom and Gomorrah to destruction because their people did evil in the sight of the Lord. However, God saved Lot and his family, the only just residents. God cautioned Lot, his wife, and his daughters against looking back at Sodom as they escaped. Lot's wife disobeyed this command, and she was turned into a pillar of salt.

6. Instant Death (Acts 5:1–11): In the early days of the Church, the faithful would sell property and give the proceeds of the sale to the Apostles. The Apostles would distribute the money to those in need. Ananias and Sapphira, a husband and wife, sold a piece of property, but kept back part of the proceeds for their own use while accepting the admiration of the community for their donation. When confronted separately with their lie, both Ananias and Sapphira dropped dead — literally.

5. Flood (Genesis 6–9): The early chapters of the Book of Genesis tell of a time when human beings became so evil that God decided that he needed to start again from scratch. He sent a flood caused by forty days and forty nights of rain. The flood destroyed all living things on earth — except for the occupants of the ark, Noah, his family, and the animals they had brought with them. Noah, unlike other human beings, was not wicked, so the Lord saved him. The devastation of the flood was so great that God promised that never again would he destroy all living things.

4. Expulsion from Eden (Genesis 3): Adam and Eve violated God's instruction not to eat the fruit of the tree of knowledge of good and evil, and they were punished for this offense. They were expelled from the Garden of Eden and made subject to death. Adam was condemned to work to till the soil, and Eve was cursed with pain in childbirth. No matter how sweet the fruit, it could not be worth so bitter a punishment.

3. The Ten Plagues (Exodus 7–11): God sent Moses and Aaron to Pharaoh to ask that he release the Israelites from their slavery in Egypt. Pharaoh refused, reluctant to lose his labor force on the command of a God he did not know. God sent ten plagues upon the Egyptians to try to convince Pharaoh to let the Israelites go. The first nine plagues disrupted life and must have been dreadfully uncomfortable. The Nile was turned to blood, rendering it unusable. The land was overrun with frogs, locusts, flies, and gnats. The livestock were afflicted with a pestilence. The people were afflicted with boils. The land was pelted with hail and covered with unending darkness. Yet none of these plagues was sufficient to change Pharaoh's mind. The final plague was the death of the first-born, both human and animal, of every house of Egypt. This final devastating blow convinced Pharaoh to let the Israelites go.

2. Crucifixion (Matthew 27; Mark 15; Luke 23; John 19): Crucifixion was the worst punishment inflicted by the Roman Empire. After being scourged, the condemned man was forced to carry the cross to the place of execution where he was stripped and tied or nailed to the cross. He would die, sometimes after days, from blood loss, exposure, shock, and suffocation. It was a humiliating and painful way to die. Jesus accepted the pain and humiliation to redeem even the worst of human experiences so that we could enjoy eternal life with God.

1. Eternal Damnation: Eternal damnation — eternal separation from the love of God — is the ultimate punishment. It is the unending and hopeless fate of those who reject God and who choose evil instead of striving for good. God is always willing to forgive, but human beings must choose to repent. Following the Evil One means following him into hell and eternal death.

TALK TO THE ANIMALS

The Bible is the story of God's relationship with human beings. But even though human beings take center stage, animals play important roles as actors and as symbols. (Note: The biblical citations below are representative rather than exhaustive lists of the references to the various animals.)

10. Dogs (Tobit 6; Psalm 22; Mark 7:27–28; Luke 17:21): With the exception of Tobiah's faithful dog who travels with Tobiah and Raphael, dogs are typically depicted as scavengers, eating table scraps, licking the sores of beggars, and surrounding those who are in desperate straits. Dogs are often associated with the poor and humble, those to whom we are called to offer compassion.

9. Animals of the Plagues (Exodus 7–10): As part of the effort to convince Pharaoh to release the Israelites from slavery, Moses calls down ten plagues on the Egyptian people. Four of these plagues involve animals: frogs, gnats, flies, and locusts. While the presence of these animals is not uncommon, a supernatural quantity of these animals marked the plagues. The overabundance of these animals damaged crops and made life unbearable for the Egyptians, though none of these plagues was enough to break Pharaoh's resistance.

8. The Raven and the Dove (Genesis 8): After forty days of the flood, Noah released a raven to see if the waters had lessened. The raven flew back and forth across the land until the waters dried off from the earth. Later, Noah released a dove to see if the land had dried. Initially, the dove came back. The next time, the dove returned with a leaf in its beak, indicating that trees were flourishing once again. Finally, the dove failed to return when released. It had built its nest on the renewed earth.

7. Pigs (Mark 5 and Luke 15): When Jesus cured a demoniac in the Gadaerene (or Gerasene) territory, he sent the demons into a herd of pigs. When the Prodigal Son was broke and facing a famine, he took work feeding pigs. In both of these cases, the pigs were clear indicators that the action had moved outside the land of Israel. The Jewish people would never have raised pigs because pigs were unclean. Only foreigners would have included pigs among their livestock. Yet Jesus never judged these "outsiders" harshly.

6. Bulls (Exodus 24; Numbers 19; Amos 4): Bulls were important animals of sacrifice, used in ceremonies of particular importance, such as the acceptance of the covenant. Similarly, the ashes left after the sacrifice of a red heifer were used by the Israelites for purification. In another context, Amos compared the rich who ignored the needs of the poor to bulls being fattened for slaughter.

5. Snake (Genesis 3): The snake appeared in Eden, using its guile to convince Adam and Eve to disobey the Lord's command and eat the fruit of the tree of knowledge of good and evil. For his role in this first sin, God cursed the snake, condemning it to crawl about on its belly and to be in eternal hostility with the human race. Thus, the snake became a symbol of evil and death.

4. Donkey (Matthew 21; Mark 11; Luke 19:28–40; John 12:12–19): The donkey is most famous for its role in Jesus' triumphant entry into Jerusalem. The disciples borrow a donkey for Jesus to ride as he comes into the city in the days before his death. Jesus comes as a strange sort of king, riding a humble beast of burden rather than a horse. By his actions, Jesus shows that, in his kingdom, to reign is to serve.

3. Fattened Calf (Luke 15): Fattening a calf takes time, attention, and a commitment of feed. The fattened calf was destined to be slaughtered to create a special meal. When the Prodigal Son returned home, his father welcomed him with great joy, throwing a huge party and killing the fattened calf to serve to the guests. The fattened calf was a symbol of the father's abundant joy in his son's return.

2. Sheep (see especially Ezekiel 34; Luke 15; John 10): Sheep are one of the most commonly mentioned animals in the Bible because of the important symbol of the shepherd. Ezekiel chastises the corrupt leaders of Israel, comparing them to shepherds who exploit their flocks. In contrast, God is compared to a shepherd who gently cares for his flock and who goes out to search for a lost sheep, bringing it home with great joy once found. Jesus calls himself the good shepherd, the one who guides and protects the sheep in his fold; knowing them, loving them, and calling them by name.

1. Lamb (Exodus 12; John 1:29; Revelation 5–22): The lamb has a very special place in Scripture. It is the blood of the Passover lamb that marks the Israelites' doorposts, protecting them from the final plague, the death of the firstborn. Later, John identifies Jesus as the Lamb of God, the Lamb whose blood will save human beings from death, opening the gates of eternal life. Christ, the victorious Lamb, is depicted in the Book of Revelation, ruling over the new Jerusalem.

THE FORTIETH LIST

In many ways, this is the most important list in this book, because this list will arise from your own interaction with God's Word. Think back on the Bible stories you have read or heard throughout your life. Which of these stories have touched your heart? challenged you? comforted you? taught you an important lesson? Choose ten of these stories and list them here, noting why each story is meaningful to you.

10. _____

_____

_____

_____

9. _____

_____

_____

_____

8. _____

_____

_____

_____

7. _____

_____

_____

_____

6. _____

_____

_____

_____

5. _____

_____

_____

_____

4. _____

_____

_____

_____

3. _____

_____

_____

_____

2. _____

_____

_____

_____

1. _____

_____

_____

_____

ACKNOWLEDGMENTS

It's always dangerous to start saying thank you, because you can never thank everyone who helped you complete a project like this. However, I do need to single out a few people whose specific support of this project cannot go unrecognized.

First, my thanks go to Greg Erlandson, publisher of Our Sunday Visitor, who first came to me with the idea of writing this book. Bert Ghezzi, my editor, remained patient and supportive through all my "idea of the day" emails.

Paul Henderson and Helen Osman, my supervisors at the USCCB, made it possible for me to undertake this project. It is a pleasure and honor to work for you.

I appreciate the assistance of the members of the Catholic Biblical Association who embraced the project and made excellent suggestions in our conversations. Any mistakes are mine.

My gratitude to all my friends who, through their words and emails, offered me encouragement and support, especially, Lisa, Jenn, Vicki, Deb, and Noreen.

Hershey, my rescue terrier, is more faithful than Tobiah's dog and was very good about telling me when it was time to stop writing and take a walk.

I am enormously indebted to my family. My sisters Carol Ann and Kathy asked about progress and kept believing I would finish.

Without my parents, this book, quite simply, would not have been possible. They introduced me to faith and the Bible. They have always been my best teachers and my role models. I love you. This book is for you.